The Minority Peoples of China

The Minority Peoples of China

by Margaret Rau

Illustrated with photographs

Julian Messner   New York

Copyright © 1982 by Margaret Rau

Published by Julian Messner, a Simon & Schuster
Division of Gulf & Western Corporation,
Simon & Schuster Building,
1230 Avenue of the Americas,
New York, New York 10020.

JULIAN MESSNER and colophon are trademarks of
Simon & Schuster, registered in the U.S. Patent
and Trademark Office.

Manufactured in the United States of America.

Design by Virginia M. Soulé

Library of Congress Cataloging in Publication Data

Rau, Margaret.
    The minority peoples of China.

    Includes index.
    Summary: Describes the lives and customs of some
of the fifty-six minority groups of China, most of
whom occupy mountain regions or live along the
borders.
    1. Minorities—China—Juvenile literature.
2. China—Race relations—Juvenile literature.
[1. Minorities—China.   2. China—Social life and
customs.   I. Title.
DS730.R38   305.8'00951   82-15311
ISBN 0-671-41545-X   AACR2

CONTENTS

Messner Books by Margaret Rau

The Minority Peoples of China
Our World: The People's Republic of China
The People of New China
The Yangtze River
The Yellow River

The
Minority
Peoples
of China

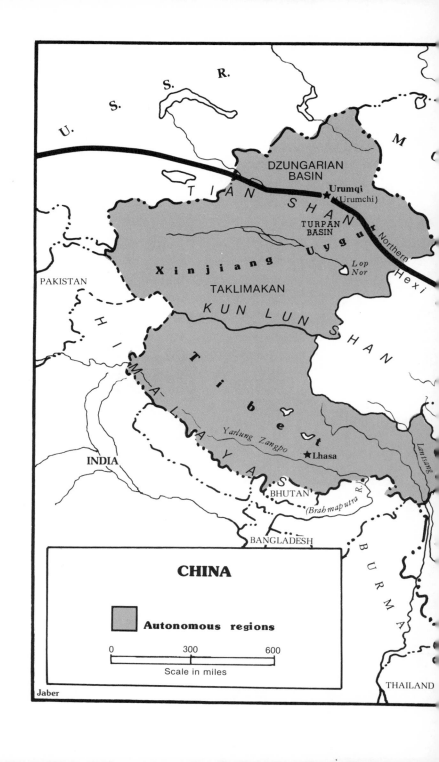

U. S. S. R.

DZUNGARIAN
BASIN

TIAN SHAN

★Urumqi
(Urumchi)

TURPAN
BASIN

Xinjiang Uygu

Northern

Hexi

Lop
Nor

PAKISTAN

TAKLIMAKAN

KUN LUN SHAN

HIMALAYAS

Tibet

Yarlung Zangpo

★Lhasa

INDIA

BHUTAN

(Brahmaputra R.)

Lantsang

BANGLADESH

BURMA

CHINA

Autonomous regions

| 0 | 300 | 600 |

Scale in miles

Jaber

THAILAND

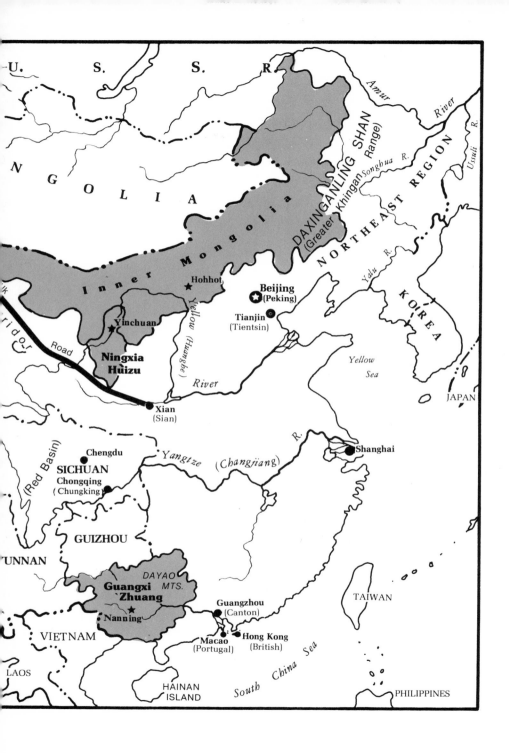

INTRODUCTION

The majority of the people who live in China are known as Han Chinese. But China also has some fifty-six minority nationalities, most of whom occupy the mountainous regions or live along the country's borders.

In the south there are numerous minorities who look very much like Han Chinese. They are related to the peoples of Burma and Southeast Asia. Once these peoples lived on the plains, which in early times were covered with dense subtropical forests. Their culture was more primitive than that of the Han Chinese who were centered in the valley of the Yellow River and the North China plain.

As the Chinese nation expanded, pioneer farmers accompanied by soldiers moved south to populate the land. They felled the forests and planted rice fields, crowding out the earlier peoples who had to retreat into the mountains. Here they lived a harsh life and there was bad feeling between them and the Han Chinese.

Far to the north in Manchuria, or the Northeast Region as it is known today, lived other tribes. They were fierce nomads who roamed the plains and mountain forests of the cold north. Most of them were Manchus who in 1644 marched south to conquer the Han Chinese. Once in Peking the Manchus adopted Chinese culture and language. In the centuries that followed there were many inter-marriages between Han Chinese and Manchus. And today fewer than 50 people even remember the old Manchu tongue, while Manchu ways and customs have completely died out. The Manchus are no longer even considered a minority people. But there are other tribes who have lived for centuries in the isolated places of the Northeast Region. These peoples still cling to their customs, and so are numbered among China's minorities.

To the west lies Mongolia, which was also inhabited by various nomad tribes. Through the centuries, wave after wave of these fierce raiders would sweep southward into the lands of the Han Chinese. They would burn villages, massacre the people in them or carry them away as slaves. They would turn their fields into pasturage for their flocks and herds. Sometimes the nomads were strong enough to set up kingdoms in China. Greatest of the Mongol conquerors was Kublai Khan, who invaded China and established his capital at Peking in 1279. Today Mongolia is divided into two parts which are called Outer Mongolia or the People's Republic of Mongolia, and Inner Mongolia. Inner Mongolia is now part of China and the Mongolians who live there are one of the country's important minorities.

The minority peoples known as Hui are scattered about China. But the greatest numbers of them are concentrated in the northwest. The Hui look, dress and act like Han Chinese. They speak the Han language. They are the descendants of Arab traders who came to live in China centuries ago and intermarried with the Chinese. They are considered a minority because they follow many of the Moslem practices and customs of their Arab ancestors.

Still further west lies the desert country of Xinjiang (Sinkiang) where several other minorities live. Principal among them are the Uygurs and Kazaks. All the other minorities in China have a common ancestral strain and share the same facial characteristics. But the people who inhabit Xinjiang look different. They are related to the peoples who live in Central Asia and are of Turkic stock.

For centuries Xinjiang has played an important role between east and west. Down its corridor, hemmed in by towering mountains, new ideas and products passed to and fro along the Old Silk Roads. In the reign of the great emperor, Han Wu Di (40–87 B.C.) the rulers of the little oases kingdoms appealed to the Chinese court for protection against the raids of the fierce nomads who lived in the mountains above them. Han Wu Di began the practice of establishing garrisons along the Old Silk Roads. Eventually Xinjiang became a part of China. But during the latter part of the Ching Dynasty, when the Empire was weak, China lost control of the territory, which split up into warring factions. Then both Russia and Great Britain began sending scouting expeditions and spies into the area with the idea of annexing it for themselves.

South of Xinjiang lies the high plateau of Tibet, home of the Tibetan minority people. In its long history Tibet has sometimes been under Chinese control and sometimes independent. At one period a fierce Tibetan tribe was able to conquer part of China and establish its kingdom there. When the Ching Empire was strong, the Tibetan ruler, the Fifth Dalai Lama, appealed to Peking for protection and Tibet became a protectorate of China. But as the Ching Empire weakened and could no longer protect Tibet, both Great Britain and Russia began showing increasing interest in Tibet. Great Britain was able to annex part of the region along Tibet's boundary with India and add it to that country, which was then her colony.

After the People's Republic was founded in 1949, Inner Mongolia, Xinjiang, and Tibet were all drawn back under Chinese rule. Wishing to foster good relations with her minority peoples, the new government gave the status of Autonomous Region to those areas which contained large concentrations of a minority people. Smaller areas were set up as Autonomous Districts.

There are five Autonomous Regions in China. The Guangxi (Kuangsi) Autonomous Region in the far south is the home of the Zhuang (Chuang), China's largest minority. The Ningxia (Ningsia) plain in China's northwest is inhabited mainly by Hui Chinese. The other three Autonomous Regions are Inner Mongolia, Xinjiang, and Tibet.

The first Constitution of the People's Republic of China guaranteed Autonomous Regions and Districts the freedom to practice their own customs, speak their own language and follow their particular religious beliefs. Minority Nationalities were also given control of their internal affairs, though under the guidance of Peking (Beijing).

However, during the ten years of the Cultural Revolution (1966-1976) these freedoms were taken away. This was a period of suffering and turmoil for the whole country under the domination of a far leftist faction. After it was overthrown in 1976, the new government began righting the wrongs done its citizens. Today it is pouring money into developing agricultural and technical skills in minority areas in order to improve conditions there. Wherever possible Han officials are being replaced by minority leaders. And minorities again have the freedom to follow their own culture, religion and customs and to use their own language.

In the following pages the lives and customs of only some of China's many minorities can be covered. But first a word of explanation about China's new form of phonetic spelling. In dealing with historical happenings and places, the old spelling is being retained. But modern-day names have been spelled the new way. However, these spellings use a system of phonetics which in some instances is so foreign to English usage that readers are likely to become confused. The following pronunciation guide should help them to arrive at the correct pronunciation.

a   Vowel as in *far*

b   Consonant as in *be*

c   Consonant as in *its*

ch Consonant as in *church*, strongly aspirated

d   Consonant as in *do*

e   Vowel as in *her*

f   Consonant as in *foot*

g   Consonant as in *go*

h   Consonant as in *her*, strongly aspirated

i   Vowel as in *eat* or as in *sir* (when in syllables beginning with c, ch, r, s, sh, z and zh)

j   Consonant as in *jeep*

k   Consonant as in *kind*, strongly aspirated

l   Consonant as in *land*

m   Consonant as in *me*

n   Consonant as in *no*

o   Vowel as in *law*

p   Consonant as in *par*, strongly aspirated

q   Consonant as in *cheek*

r   Consonant as in *right* (not rolled) or pronounced as z in *azure*

s   Consonant as in *sister*

sh Consonant as in *shore*

t   Consonant as in *top*, strongly aspirated

u   Vowel as in *too*, also as in the French *tu* or the German *München*

v   Consonant used only to produce foreign words, national minority words and local dialects

w   Semi-vowel in syllables beginning with u when not preceded by consonants, as in *want*

x   Consonant as in *she*

y   Semi-vowel in syllables beginning with i or u when not preceded by consonants, as in *yet*

z   Consonant as in *zero*

zh Consonant as in *jump*

Source: Adapted from Beijing Review

1

BAIMA LHAMO OF TIBET

Eleven-year-old Baima Lhamo lives in Lhasa, capital of Tibet, an Autonomous Region. Tibet is often called "the Roof of the World" because it is so high above sea level. The cold, inhospitable land is made up of valleys and great plateaus that range from 5000 feet above sea level to 20,000 feet. The valleys and plateaus are ringed by mountains that tower even higher—the Himalayas to the south, the Kunluns to the north, the wild Shaluli and Great Snowy ranges to the east.

For centuries the mountain ranges have acted as barriers to isolate Tibet from the rest of the world. Even today it isn't easy to travel around the country. Some dirt highways cross Tibet, snaking over the mountains. But rock slides and snow avalanches make these roads perilous during much of the year. Airplanes service the capital city of Lhasa when the weather is clear. The airfield is only a three-mile-long concrete runway lying between two mountain ranges.

Lhasa itself stands in a high fertile valley some 12,000 feet above sea level. Though there are only about 140 frost-free days a year it can produce fine crops of chinko barley, buckwheat, rye, peas, winter wheat and cabbage. The valley is watered by the Yarlung Zangbo

River and is surrounded by craggy mountains which rise above the timberline where no trees grow.

Many people could not endure the high altitudes and thin air of Tibet. But Baima, who has grown up here, has developed much larger lungs than children who live in the lowlands. Her blood contains many more red blood cells which enable her body to make full use of the scanty oxygen. Her rich blood gives her cheeks a ruddy glow. She is a sturdy little girl with a round face and sparkling black eyes and hair that reaches her waist.

Baima's home is on a side street in the newer part of Lhasa. It is made of stone and adobe, a kind of brick made from mud and straw. There are no trees to provide lumber for wooden houses. Baima shares a room with her grandmother and younger brother, Manba, who is seven. Their beds are couches, covered with felt blankets in the daytime. The front room serves as a bedroom for Baima's mother and

Flowers brighten this adobe home in Lhasa.

father. Baima's older brother, his wife and three-year-old daughter live in a small room across a little courtyard.

An electric bulb hangs from a cord in the center of the living room. The light is powered by a small generator which Baima's father turns off in the daytime to save energy.

The kitchen is dark. Its walls are grimed with soot from the big potbellied cooking stove that burns both wood and grassroot blocks. The blocks are cut out of the earth and dried. The tangle of roots embedded in the soil make a smoky fire. In the courtyard a small brazier or firepot is used as an extra stove.

Now it is late September and the weather is dry. What rain there is usually comes in the summer, though very little falls even then. Most of the monsoons, seasonal rains, coming up from India are stopped by the towering Himalayas.

Sometimes winds, often freezing, howl over the plateau, filling the world with a sea of dust. Then Baima puts on a face mask to keep from breathing in the stinging sand that parches her throat and makes her chest ache every time she draws a breath.

But now the weather is clear, almost summery still. Out in the fields teams of women walk through fields of ripened chinko barley, slashing at the stalks with their sharp scythes. As they walk they sing, swinging in rhythm to the music.

In some fields the harvest is already in and the fallow earth is being plowed by oxen or yaks. The yak, which is related to the American bison and somewhat resembles it, is an awkward-looking shaggy animal.

There are more than twelve million yaks in Tibet. Yaks are among the few species of animal that can endure high altitudes. Yaks serve the Tibetans well. They are used to plow the fields, to carry burdens, to provide milk, yogurt, butter and meat. Boats made of yak

17

Yaks are used for plowing.

skin ply the Yarlung Zangbo river, serving as ferries for people and produce. Yak manure is plastered on the walls of farmhouses till it dries into cakes which are then used for fuel. Yak hair is woven into a thick material which keeps out cold, snow and rain. It is made into long cloaks or *shubas* which keep the Tibetans warm during the winters when the temperature drops below zero.

Herds of yak, along with cattle and sheep, are raised on the higher plateaus where the growing season is too short and the land too poor for farming. The fall is bringing snow flurries to the mountain valleys where the animals have been passing the summer, and the herdsmen are starting to move them to lower pastures.

The Lhamo family is also preparing for winter. They are stocking up on logs which come by truck from the foot of the Himalayas where great forests grow. The logs have to be brought in early, before ice and snow block the roads.

Fuel in Lhasa is expensive because it has to be trucked in over the mountains. So the family uses the logs only for cooking. The house is not heated even when temperatures drop below zero Fahrenheit. To keep warm, the family put on more layers of sweaters and eventually their long, heavy shubas.

Some members of Baima's family, along with several other people in the neighborhood, have formed a small cooperative to produce and sell products. There are two sewing machines on which they make children's clothes. Some of the women turn sheep's wool into yarn on old-fashioned spindles. Then they knit the yarn into vests and sweaters and even woolen shubas. The men have tools with which they fashion wooden bowls, butter buckets and yak saddles.

The cooperative sells its products in the open market in the old section of town known as the Old City. They are able to make a fair living at it. Tibet is a poor country and none of the Tibetans are really well-to-do. But the Lhamos are better off than most.

In Lhasa the day begins at 6:30 A.M. when loudspeakers blare out the lively strains of a Chinese song. The martial music wakens the soldiers stationed in their barracks on craggy Iron Hill where once a monastery stood. It rouses the people who live in apartment buildings in the suburbs. It brings Baima and Manba out of their dreams with a start.

Even in summertime the sky is still velvet black at that hour. The stars sparkle like diamonds. The sun will not rise for more than an hour. China operates under one time zone—Beijing time. But Beijing at this hour is already light. In far western Lhasa everyone has to get up in pitch darkness.

Baima and the rest of the family sit down to breakfast. No fire is

19

needed to prepare this meal. Water has been kept hot in thermos bottles from the night before. It is mixed with tea and butter to make yak butter tea, a rich, thick, somewhat rancid-tasting soup of which the Tibetans are very fond. The family also eats *tsamba*, a strong smelling paste made of roasted barley flour. Baima and her family pick up a glob of the paste, roll it into a ball, dip it into the buttered tea and eat it.

After the meal is over the family scatters. Baima's sister-in-law gets on her bicycle and heads off for the carpet factory where she works. Her husband leaves too. He is employed in a farm machinery plant. There are a number of other small factories in Lhasa's suburbs.

A little later the rest of the family goes to the cooperative. Only Grandmother, Baima, Manba and the baby stay behind. The older children will soon be starting off for school.

Once only a religious education was possible in Tibet. Now almost every district in Lhasa has its own primary and elementary school. There are also some high schools and several colleges in the Region. School is free, but children do not have to attend, and many do not.

Grandmother helps Baima and Manba get ready. She scrubs Baima's face and hands with a cloth dipped in a basin of water drawn from the community faucet outside. The water is cold, for it comes from the melting snow and ice of the high mountains. Baima grits her teeth as her grandmother scrubs. Manba is not so patient. He squeals until the job is done.

This is as much bathing as the children will have. Fuel is too scarce to use for heating bath water. And bathing in freezing water might encourage a cold which could quickly turn into pneumonia at this high altitude.

The sun has risen by the time Baima and Manba are ready to set off for school. The children carry little green knapsacks containing their schoolbooks. Manba is just learning to read. Baima studies

20

Bringing home firewood
they have collected.

arithmetic, history, and politics. Her books are written in the Tibetan language, which looks like the Sanskrit used in India, on the other side of the Himalayas. Baima is also learning Han Chinese, China's official language.

Outside their gate the children enter a dusty street lined by the outside walls of houses like their own. Here and there other children with knapsacks over their shoulders are emerging from doorways and Baima and Manba stick out their tongues at them—this is the Tibetan greeting.

Most of the children on Baima's street do not go to school. These children are dressed in ragged dirty clothes. Their faces are grimy and their uncombed, tangled hair sticks up in all directions. They are having a lot of fun, laughing and screaming as they race up and down the

A side street in old Lhasa.

dusty lane. Manba wishes he could stay home and play with them, but Grandmother will not allow the children of her family to grow up ignorant.

Grandmother appears much older than her sixty-one years. Her lips are sunken over toothless gums. Deep lines seam her face. She is stooped and very thin. One leg is crippled from a beating she received in her childhood. Grandmother was a slave then. In the old days most Tibetans were either serfs or slaves whose masters could do as they pleased with them. These masters were the noblemen, the monks, and the government. Between them they held ninety-six percent of the land.

Once the people had so little to eat that they often gave their male children away to the big Buddhist monasteries, or lamaseries as they are called in Tibet. The children became hard-working servant lamas. They had to follow the Buddhist religious rules, which did not permit lamas to marry. But at least they could eat, and as the years went by more and more young boys entered the lamaseries. Three-fourths of all Tibetan males became lamas. Today many of the former servant lamas have married and have families. And most of the lamaseries have been closed or destroyed, though a number are now being renovated and reopened.

The Potala, the fortress palace of Lhasa, stands on a 700-foot-high cliff, overlooking the city. Its cream- and maroon-colored walls, brightly painted wooden pillars, rafters and beams topped by gilded tile roofs and golden steeples seem to grow out of the cliff itself. Indeed, the name of the palace is the same as the mountain: Potala, which means "Buddha's Mountain," or "the Mountain of God." For centuries Potala has been the home of the Dalai Lamas or priest-rulers of Tibet. Dalai Lama means "Ocean of Wisdom." Tibetan tradition says that all the Dalai Lamas are really just one person, known as a

The Potala.

Living Buddha. Each time a Dalai Lama dies, it is said, his soul is quickly reborn into a new body.

After the death of a Dalai Lama, the Council of Lamas searched for the newborn baby into which they believed the Dalai Lama's soul had entered. They always looked for a baby born in a cow shed. When such a child was discovered the lamas would present him with a number of objects, among which were some of the late Dalai Lama's personal things. If the boy chose these things correctly, the lamas proclaimed him the new Dalai Lama and brought him back to Lhasa to live in the Potala. They gave him religious training and when he reached eighteen years of age he took over the political and spiritual rule of Tibet.

Today there is a Dalai Lama—the fourteenth—but he is no longer living in the Potala. After the People's Republic of China was founded in 1949 the Chinese army entered Tibet. The Dalai Lama went to Beijing where he signed a pact with the new government. The Dalai Lama was to continue ruling his country's internal affairs, while the Beijing government was to handle foreign policy. This continued until 1956 when the Tibetans rebelled against the Chinese. A number of Tibetans were killed before the rebellion was put down. The Dalai Lama, accompanied by some 90,000 followers, fled across the Himalayas into India.

The Potala has now been converted into a museum. But the Dalai Lama's living quarters wait undisturbed for his return. The Chinese government has said he may come back either as a visitor or a resident. As a resident he may take up his spiritual leadership again, but the Chinese will not permit him to return as political ruler of Tibet.

Younger Tibetans for the most part do not follow the Buddhist faith, but they would like to have the Dalai Lama come back. To them he is the representative of national independence.

Baima's grandmother, along with many others who are still devout Buddhists, also yearns for the return of the Dalai Lama. Once a day the old woman walks slowly around the base of the Potala twirling her prayer wheel. The wheel contains several strips of paper on which have been written prayers. Grandmother believes that every time the wheel revolves the prayers are being recited so she does not need to speak them aloud.

Grandmother also stops to tie prayer strips onto several of the shrubs that grow on the Potala grounds. Hundreds of prayer strips already float from these shrubs. The worshippers are sure that when the wind flutters the strips, the prayers on them are being said.

Sometimes Baima accompanies her grandmother to the Tibetan Institute of Medicine which is in a tall, whitewashed building in the

Prayer strips flutter in breeze.

Old City at the foot of the Potala. The Institute is staffed by traditional Tibetan doctors who use herbal medicines and also practice acupuncture. Acupuncture is a method of healing which uses needles inserted in the body in key places.

Though there are several modern hospitals in Lhasa, Grandmother prefers the old way, where horoscopes are read and astrological charts are drawn up for each patient. Many other elderly people come here, too, and Grandmother is likely to meet some of her friends. They exchange greetings—several just sticking out their tongues, others giving a hug while pressing foreheads together.

Opposite the hospital, peasants and herdsmen have set up canvas tents. They have come to sell their produce and livestock in the open market in the Old City, and they will stay several days.

Baima is always fascinated by the Old City. The narrow, winding

A marketplace in Lhasa.

streets are lined by massive three-story-high stone buildings. The buildings slope slightly backward in the old style. Pots of flowers line the sills of the upper windows.

Swarms of people crowd through the narrow streets: peasants in worn, dirty shubas, their faces seamed by wind and cold and hard work—young mothers carrying babies on their backs—old men shuffling along, felt hats pulled low over their foreheads and long woolen gowns swishing. There are wild herdsmen, their black hair streaming under their broad felt hats. Priests in maroon—a deep, rich red—robes stand, quietly telling their beads. Young women from the countryside stride along in old-style, voluminous felt petticoats and shubas. Their long black hair is plaited in dozens of tiny black braids interwoven with gay ribbons. And there are soldiers wearing green uniforms and caps with red stars. Approximately 300,000 soldiers are stationed in Tibet, about 100,000 in Lhasa itself.

Everywhere people are selling things—to get a little extra, much-needed money. They may be family possessions—a turquoise bracelet or coral necklace, for the Tibetans dearly love jewelry, or an elaborately carved prayer wheel or a silver box. With a prayer strip inside, the box can be worn around the neck, doing double duty as ornament and amulet to ward off evil.

Produce is also for sale: bundles of little green onions, heaps of cabbages, containers holding great lumps of waxy yak butter. There are heaps of raw yak meat brought from the stockyards on the outskirts of the city.

Some stalls display cheap modern trinkets, toiletries, children's shoes and clothes, including babies' padded pants with the crotch cut out of them. Babies in China wear this kind of pants until they learn to use a toilet. The Lhamos' cooperative displays its goods here, and

Everywhere, people are selling things.

Baima is pleased when she sees a crowd of people around the table on which the articles are laid out.

Whenever Grandmother goes to the Old City she always visits the Jokan, (formerly spelled Jokhang) the oldest and most sacred monastery in all Tibet. The Jokan, which means "temple of the Sakyamuni Buddha," houses the bronze statue brought from China by the little Tang Dynasty Princess, Wen Cheng, when she came to be the bride of King Songzan Ganbu (formerly spelled Songtsen Gampo) in A.D. 641.

The Jokan is open for worship three times a week. Even on the days it is closed, Grandmother and other fervent Buddhists stretch out full length on the ground, worshipping before the closed gates. Then they circle the temple, halting at intervals to lie down again on the ground, facing the place where the Buddha is housed.

When the temple is open, more than a thousand pilgrims may

Praying before the Jokan.

come to worship. A lama sits at the open gate collecting a small fee from each worshipper: ten fen, which amounts to about seven cents in United States money. The donations are used for the upkeep of the monastery.

Most of the pilgrims carry lighted butter lamps or thermos flasks filled with melted yak butter. They leave their lamps on one of the altars or pour the melted butter from the flasks into the chalices already there.

Baima, who sometimes comes to the temple with her grandmother, always has a strange feeling as she enters the central hall. Yak butter candles cast their flickering lights over the rich wall decorations and brocade hangings. All around, through the smoky radiance, thirty-foot-high gilded statues look down on the pilgrims. There is a strange, pungent odor caused by more than a thousand years of burning butter. Baima's feet slip as she approaches the altars, for the floor there is black with ancient grease.

The procession moves forward, weaving through the various shrines, chanting ancient Buddhist prayers, until it reaches the statue brought by Princess Wen Cheng. At last Grandmother and Baima stand before it. Gold leaf covers the great bronze image which is dressed in satin robes richly ornamented with turquoises, pearls, rubies, emeralds. A massive jeweled crown rests on the Buddha's head.

Baima's parents no longer believe in Buddhism. Baima herself has learned at school that there is no powerful Buddha. But when Grandmother reverently prostrates herself before the statue, Baima joins her on the grimy floor. Beneath the Buddha's serene gaze she feels something of the religious awe that has been with her grandmother ever since she was a little slave girl and had only her faith in the Buddha's mercy to comfort her.

2

THE UYGURS

While Baima Lhamo lives on a plateau so high it is called "the Roof of the World," Murat Amat lives in one of the lowest depressions on earth. His home is in the Turpan basin which lies in the Autonomous Region of Xinjiang (formerly spelled Sinkiang), in China's far northwest. Xinjiang, which makes up one sixth of China's territory, is desert country.

The Northern Silk Road, an ancient trading route, passed through the Turpan depression where Murat Amat lives. The basin lies in the heart of the towering Tian Shan mountain range. Enclosed by mountains, the desert basin becomes a baking cauldron in summer when temperatures may rise to more than 120 degrees Fahrenheit, making it the hottest place in China.

In the days of the Old Silk Routes, Grecian, Persian, Arabic, Indian and Chinese traders passed to and fro through Turpan. Each culture left its mark in sculptures, cities and religious buildings.

Today Turpan's glory is gone. Only some 140,000 people live here, scattered throughout the farming oases. Clusters of yellow adobe houses lie among gardens of spreading melon vines, of cotton and

The desert basin, Flaming Mountain in distance.

wheat fields, vineyards and fruit orchards. Around each oasis stretch barren sands and shifting dunes mixed with grey pebbled plains. The plains are called *gobi deserts* because *gobi* means pebble. For centuries howling winds have scoured away all the soil from this rubbled grey and black wilderness.

Murat is used to the dry desert weather because he has lived here all his life. He is a thin wiry boy with brown wavy hair and dark round eyes. His nose has a high bridge and his skin is olive-colored. He and his family and neighbors do not look at all like Tibetans or

An oasis town.

A gobi desert.

Han Chinese. This is because they come of Turkic stock and are related to the people of Central Asia and the Near East—the people of Samarkand and Kabul, Jerusalem, Uzbek, Turkistan, Armenia and ancient Persia. Centuries ago they migrated from the west into Xinjiang. They call themselves Uygurs.

Murat dresses in T-shirt and trousers or short pants in the hot weather. His mother and sisters wear long pants under their dresses. Their hair hangs in thick braids down their backs. Old and young, men and women, all wear embroidered caps of silk or velvet.

They are very proud of these caps. The young people wear caps embroidered with bright bold colors. Sober black caps with white embroidery are preferred by older people, such as Murat's grandfather who looks very dignified with his white hair and long white beard.

Murat's home, like all the houses in the village, is made of large adobe bricks. The walls are more than a foot thick. This makes the rooms cooler in summer and warmer in winter. The roofs are almost flat. There is no need for steep slopes to shed rain, because the rainfall here is less than six inches a year.

Murat shares a room with his older brother Aziz. A hard platform of adobe has been built against one wall. It is covered with several blankets and quilts. This is the boys' bed. Murat's older and younger sisters, Imsahan and Ruzihan, sleep on a similar adobe bed in another small room. Grandfather has a little room of his own. The living room has a large platform bed on which Murat's parents sleep. In the daytime the bed serves as a couch. The living room walls are decorated with pictures taken from calendars. There is a small table with two chairs beside it, and a chest where clothes are stored.

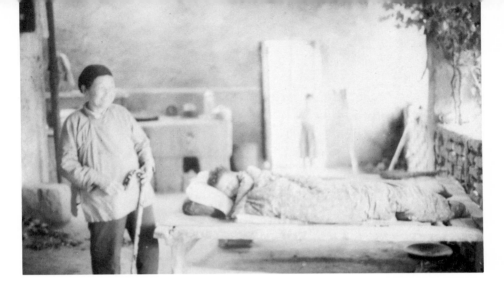

This platform bed can also serve as a couch.

Like everyone else in the Turpan basin, the Amats have built an arbor on one side of their house. Thick-trunked grapevines grow over the trellises of the arbor, casting their speckled shade below. When the weather is hot, the Amats like to eat their meals in the shade of the arbor.

The grape arbor brings welcome shade.

The Amats sit on mats spread around a low table. There is always plenty of food—fruit in season, grapes or melons usually, then mounds of fried cakes, called *nang*. The nang are so hard they must be dipped in tea before eating. There are also deep-fried ribbonlike wheat strips and sesame-coated wheat rods, and of course vegetables: eggplant and peas or huge cabbages. Sometimes there is cheese. The meat dishes are all mutton.

Not a single pig is to be seen in Murat's village. This is because all the people there belong to the Moslem religion which bans the eating of pork. But in the Amat family only Grandfather is a devout Moslem. When the call for prayer rings out from the minaret in the village square he pauses in whatever he is doing and turns worshipfully toward the Holy City of Mecca, far away to the west in Saudi Arabia. One day he hopes to make a pilgrimage there.

Though the rest of the Amats are not so religious, they like to attend services at the Sugong Ta mosque on Moslem festival days.

A mosque in Turpan.

These are a big event in the lives of the people of Turpan, because they give everyone a chance to meet friends and relatives from other villages. Of course people dress in their best and put on their most elegant caps for the occasion.

When all the Amats are ready to go to the mosque, Murat's father and older brother harness the family donkeys to the large wooden cart. Donkeys and carts are the chief method of transportation in the basin. As soon as the donkeys are harnessed, the whole family climbs aboard the cart and the donkeys set off to the rhythm of the clanging bells around their necks. When the donkeys slow down, Murat's father keeps them moving by flicking a little whip over their heads.

The cart is equipped with rubber tires but still the going is rough,

Transportation by donkey cart and bicycle.

Roads are little more than ruts.

for the road is rutted. The Amats are bounced and shaken to and fro but they are used to this.

As they near the mosque they begin encountering other worshippers. Some are riding in carts, others are sitting astride donkeys, or trudging on foot. They are all headed for the mosque.

Near the mosque, donkeys are tethered and families enter the building. Here men and women divide to worship in separate rooms. After the services, they will mingle again, exchanging news and socializing.

The Moslem festivals are a welcome break in the hard life of the Turpan farmers. Once the fields were tilled individually. But since the founding of the People's Republic of China the Uygurs have been encouraged to pool their resources and work the land together. This makes it easier to do battle against the desert.

The villages are run by elected committees which handle local affairs. Each family is made responsible for a certain portion of the land. It is given a quota which it must fulfil. If it manages the land so well that the harvest exceeds the quota, the family is allowed to sell the surplus on the open market and keep the proceeds for itself. It also receives its share of money from the sale of its quota of grain to the government after taxes and various small fees for medical care, farm implements and schools have been paid.

In addition, every family has its own private plot where it grows vegetables either to sell in the village marketplace or to use at home. The families may own several animals, too. The Amat family has five sheep—two rams and three ewes. The sheep are shorn yearly and Murat's mother uses the wool to stuff the bed quilts she makes for her family's use. When the rams mate with the ewes and lambs are produced, an older animal may be killed for food. The family wouldn't dream of sacrificing so small a creature as a lamb.

Much of the work of the Turpan farmers consists of getting water for irrigation purposes. All the water is underground and has to be raised to the surface before it can be used. At the same time the water cannot be exposed to the hot sun for long because it would quickly evaporate. So horizontal tunnels, called *karez*, are dug underground. At intervals the tunnels are broken by shafts. The water is pumped through these shafts up into surface canals which crisscross the fields and flow into a web of irrigation ditches.

The idea of digging underground tunnels was brought from Persia more than a thousand years ago. It came down the Old Silk Road

Bathing the baby in a karez.

along with the many western fruits and plants such as grapes, pomegranates, walnuts, and cotton.

Today some nine hundred karezes irrigate the oases in the Turpan basin. One of the longest of them stretches from the Tian Shan mountains some thirty-one miles away. Here a reservoir has been built to catch the runoff from melting snows. For almost twenty-five miles the water is channeled through a tunnel in the stony gobi desert. Murat's father helped build this tunnel.

"We began in the winter, some 3000 of us," he recalls. "Oh it was bitter cold and what a howling wind! We lived in dugouts or mountain caves. It was even worse in the summer. The stones reached 130 degrees Fahrenheit. You couldn't carry them on your bare back. It took us seven years to get the job done."

Now the track of that karez is marked by a straight line of holes. These are outlet shafts even though the tunnel runs through grey gobi desert where nothing grows. The shafts are used by maintenance men who from time to time have to enter the tunnel to clean out drifting sand which can clog the karez.

Karez-digging goes on as more and more land is reclaimed from the desert. Murat's brother Aziz works on the tunnels now. He uses Father's little pick to hollow out the tunnels.

In the cold winter months work in the fields slackens. Then many of the villagers form cooperatives to weave rugs. When the rugs are sold the money will be distributed among the members of the cooperative.

As winter turns to spring there is a bustle of activity in the basin. Fields are plowed and sowed. Fertilizer is spread around the grapevines. But March through May are the worst months of the year. Windstorms blowing at more than sixty miles an hour scour the basin, driving dense curtains of sand before them. Whole dunes are lifted away. The storms threaten to bury fields and vineyards in the soft

41

drifts, and chew away at the adobe foundations of the village homes.

To protect their houses and crops the villagers have planted shelter belts of trees everywhere. Stately rows of fast-growing poplars stand tall along the banks of the canals and the sides of highways. Wherever the fields meet the desert, the trees are five deep, forming a windbreak about seventy feet wide. There are rows of poplars, elms and mulberry trees. Date palms stand vigil on the extreme fringe of desert and oasis. And fruit trees grow around the village houses.

Finally the season of winds is over. Early summer arrives and the scent of fruit blossoms fills the air. Clusters of small grapes start forming among the vines. Murat's father and brother, along with the other men of the village, begin making frames to hold up the growing weight of the grapes.

As the heat of summer builds, the flurry of activity stops and life again takes on a leisurely pace. Murat's sister Imsahan joins other young women under the shade trees. They chatter and laugh as they embroider new caps for themselves or their families.

Imsahan is making a cap which she will give to a young neighbor to show her affection for him. To give a cap as a present is to give a very special thing, just as to make fun of someone's cap is to offer that person the biggest insult possible.

Often now when the sun sets and the cool night air descends, the young men bring out their musical instruments—the tambourine, the two-stringed dutar, the five-stringed rawap and the three-stringed shala. As the orchestra strikes up people begin gathering in the large communal grape arbor.

The young women put on the traditional long, flowing Uygur costumes. Gracefully they glide out to the music of the stringed instruments and the shimmering rhythms of the tambourines, clicking the castanets in their hands. Faster and faster they whirl, their necks moving from side to side in a sinuous rhythm. It is a Uygur woman's traditional invitation to dance, and soon young men join them. To and fro, round and round they whirl and click and glide while the great desert moon rises like a lantern among the hosts of stars.

On hot summer nights Murat likes to sleep in the open courtyard beyond the grape arbor. He can use the little cot out there if Aziz does not take it first. If he can't use the cot Murat climbs up on the flat roof and spreads out his mat there, taking a padded quilt with him because the nights can turn very cold.

The moon or bright stars wheel over Murat's head, but he does not see them. As the chill sets in he wraps himself up in the quilt burying his face, ears, and finally his whole head in it. He does not waken again till the morning sun rouses him.

Lazy summer days cannot last forever and when fall comes there is fresh activity, for now the grapes are ripening. Their heavy fragrance fills the air. And Murat has only to reach up to pick what

Sleeping outside in summer seems wonderful.

he wants from the thick bunches dangling from the trellises of the family arbor.

Out in the vineyards thousands of clusters of seedless white grapes hang from their frames. Women in brightly colored dresses, their hair bound up in scarves, are picking the clusters and putting them in wicker baskets over their arms. As each basket is filled, the picker takes it to the work point recorder who stamps the picker's card. She will be paid by the quantity of grapes she gathers. One hundred and forty baskets will earn her 10 work points for which she will be paid 2 yuan, about a dollar and a half in United States money.

Other workers load the grapes onto donkey carts to be hauled off to the drying shed to be processed into raisins. Then they will be ready for export all over China and abroad.

The drying shed is built of large mud bricks arranged to leave vents in all the walls. These enable the air to circulate through the building while protecting the grapes from the direct heat of the sun. In warm weather the drying process will take a month. But if a cold snap comes along it may take two.

While the rest of the family work Murat and his little sister Ruzihan go to school. Their schoolbooks are printed in the Uygur script. Formerly the Uygurs had no written language, but with the encouragement and help of the Chinese government Uygur scholars have developed a written version of their tongue in roman letters like ours. The children also learn Han as their second language.

In school Murat studies the ancient history of Xinjiang, and learns about life on the Old Silk Road. The Silk Roads ran west from Turpan. They skirted a barren waterless land filled with great sand dunes. This is the Taklamakan, one of the harshest deserts in the world. It lies in the heart of Xinjiang.

Green oases fringe the bases of the mountains which hem in the

Taklamakan. Once long ago the oases were stopping places for caravans of camels bearing silks from China to Rome and jade and strange fruits from the west to China.

One day Murat's teacher takes the whole class to visit the ancient city of Jiaohe. Jiaohe is only ruins now. Here and there walls mark the sites of former homes. In the center of the town, behind what was once a large public square, stand the walls of a great Buddhist temple and several decaying statues.

The teacher tells the children that Jiaohe was a fortress town during the reign of the Tang emperors in the seventh century A.D. Thousands of Han soldiers came to man the fortress. Their task was to protect the caravans of camels that passed along this route going east or west. Otherwise the wild barbarian hordes who lived in the surrounding mountains would swoop down on the travelers, looting, massacring, and disrupting all travel on the Silk Road. How lonely those soldiers must have been, Murat thinks, for they had to leave their families behind in their faraway homes to the east.

Then sometime before the year 1000 the people of Jiaohe suddenly abandoned the city. But they left behind many records, which were preserved for centuries in the dry heat. The records tell only of the daily round of business transactions. They contain no hint as to why everything came to a sudden stop.

Murat wonders if he will ever know the riddle of ruined Jiaohe. Perhaps. Many secrets of the past have been unearthed here in the desert where dry air and baking sands have preserved them for so long. Maybe one day something will be brought to light that will reveal the city's hidden story. Murat wishes he could be the archaeologist to make the exciting discovery.

3

THE KAZAKS

Kamel looks around him with wide eyes as he walks beside his father down the streets of Urumqi (formerly spelled Urumchi), capital of Xinjiang. The city lies to the north of the Heavenly Mountains, the Tian Shan range, on the margins of the Dzungarian basin. Urumqi, which means "beautiful pasture lands," was once a small walled city of some 80,000 people. But for the past thirty or so years it has been growing rapidly. Today Urumqi has almost a million people and it sprawls out beyond its walls with new factories and modern buildings, a university, and a hotel.

To twelve-year-old Kamel, Urumqi is awe-inspiring. His home is in the fastnesses of the Tian Shan range where his people are herdsmen and this is his first visit to the city. Yesterday he and his father came down to sell the bags of wool that had just been shorn from the three hundred sheep they help to tend. Today they will be returning home. And Kamel will be glad of it.

How different these dry dusty plains are! Kamel is bewildered also by the crowds swarming through the streets of Urumqi. He has never seen so many people in one place before. Many look very strange to

Young girls of Urumqi.

him. There are sedate Uygurs and round-faced, boisterous Mongols, and many Han people. Most of the Hans have migrated here from eastern China in recent years and now make up about half the city's

Many different people throng the streets of Urumqi.

population. There are even some fair-skinned people with light eyes and brown hair, descendants of Russian refugees who fled to Xinjiang long ago from the oppressive rule of the Tzars. Before he is through walking the streets of Urumqi, Kamel is likely to see many of the thirteen different nationalities who live here.

Kamel himself is a Kazak. He never hears his last name because Kazaks seldom use them in everyday life. His high cheekbones, sparkling black eyes and ruddy bronze complexion give him the appearance of an American Indian boy.

The Kazaks are semi-nomad herdsmen. Raising livestock is a very important occupation in Xinjiang whose mountains provide fine pastureland for sheep, cattle, goats and horses.

Thirteen different nationalities live in Urumqi.

48

For centuries Kazaks have roamed these mountains pasturing their flocks and herds. They either worked for themselves or, more commonly, for rich owners who paid them little. Today they have united in groups called brigades which are part of a larger collective. The brigades in the collective have different chores. Some herd cattle or horses, others sheep or goats. Kamel and his father belong to one that tends sheep. The brigades manage their own affairs.

With the sale of the wool completed, father and son head out of town in their horse-drawn wagon. The road leads them through plains of rubbled rock and stretches of fertile fields surrounding small adobe villages. These are all oases, as Urumqi is itself.

Somewhere in the plain a chemical plant belches plumes of grey smoke into the clear sky. But at last the road leaves the plains behind and begins to climb the shaggy foothills of the Tian Shan. Finally the two reach the small adobe offices of the cooperative to which their brigade belongs. Kamel's father hands the money from his sale to the cooperative's secretary-treasurer who has come out to greet them. Then, leaving the cart and wagon team behind, father and son mount their own horses which they have tethered here. They canter on through glades of cottonwood and spruce trees.

Up, up, up the road goes, skirting steep canyons and tumbling brooks. Here and there it passes little clusters of familiar, white-domed tents standing under the pine trees or lining the streams. The tents are called *yurts* and they look like giant mushrooms. The yurts are made up of felt carpets stretched over wooden frames set in the ground. The door is another felt flap which is rolled up during the day and let down at night.

The interiors of the yurts are a riot of color. A brightly patterned felt carpet covers the dirt floor. Gay tapestries hang on the circular walls. Red and yellow blankets and comforters padded with wool are

Felt carpets make up the walls and door of a yurt.

piled along the edges of the walls. These make up most of the furnishings.

Presently the road Kamel and his father are following skirts the sparkling jade green waters of Heavenly Lake. It lies some 6000 feet above sea level and is fed by melting snows and mountain glaciers. Kamel and his father are almost home now. Even the horses seem to realize it and quicken their steps. At last the two canter up to their own yurt. It stands on the edge of a wide meadow among other yurts. Kamel's mother is preparing dinner outside. She is a large woman wearing a flower print dress, knee-high boots, and a kerchief about her head.

A crude framework made of crooked tree branches stands between her and the yurt. It is covered with clothes which Kamel's mother has just washed in the nearby brook. The rack is also a handy place on which to hang kitchen utensils.

The stove is a pit in the ground. In the cold weather it is dug inside the yurt. But now that it is summertime and warm, Kamel's mother likes to do her cooking outside. She is squatting over the fire, cooking pancakes in a big pot of bubbling butter which has been propped over the hole. A steaming tea kettle sits over one end of the hole. She will use the hot water to make sugary milk tea. She lifts her head a moment to greet her son and husband. Then she hurries on with the meal.

Kamel's nine-year-old sister, Biken, is squatting nearby beside a homemade cradle, rocking her baby brother gently to and fro in it. The cradle is tube-shaped, with an open side. A wooden bar runs down the length of this open side. When the family travels, a rope tied to the bar will fasten the cradle firmly to the saddle of the horse the mother is riding. Felt straps bind the baby securely in place in the cylinder, though now he is squirming and whimpering. When his whimpers turn to a howl his mother will be finished cooking and ready to nurse him.

In the deepening cool of the twilight the family squat around the fire to eat. The Kazaks are also Moslems and never touch pork. They are shepherds so there are mutton rolls for dinner with steaming cups of goat's milk, bitter but pleasing to Kamel's taste. There are hard, fried pancakes swimming in butter and there is plenty of sugary milk tea.

When night comes the famiy retires into the yurt, releasing the flap. The circular hole overhead, which remains open during the day, is then closed. The family roll themselves up in the comforters and blankets stacked against the wall and are soon asleep.

The next day Kamel and his father are off to join the other herdsmen of their brigade. Kamel enjoys being in the company of the adults. He is a good horseman and has become expert at rounding up stray sheep. He does not carry a rifle like the men who have to be always on the alert for wolves and snow leopards who prey on the sheep. Kamel is told to shout if he spots one of these predators. He never does. All the animals he sees and hears are friendly. Squirrels and birds chatter and call out from the trees. Fleet-footed red deer come quietly to the brook to drink. When Kamel is thirsty, he takes a refreshing drink of cold, fermented mare's milk out of the thermos he brings with him.

But summer cannot last forever. Toward the end of the season the committee which handles the business affairs of the brigade begins dividing the profits among the members according to the amount of work they have done. Even Kamel gets some pocket money to spend as he pleases.

And now a traveling yurt store suddenly appears among the other yurts. A counter divides the interior. Behind the counter, city goods are stacked high and two young women wait on the customers.

The Kazak women buy lengths of gaily patterned cloth for dresses. The men are interested in tobacco and jackets and boots. They will want to appear at their best for the great horse meet, which will be held soon.

When the day of the meet arrives, young and old gather from miles around. Biken is wearing her new calf-length flowered skirt and pants with a black felt vest over her blouse. The cap on her head, shaped like a pillbox, is decorated with a jaunty white feather. Even her baby brother has on a new sweater and a knitted cap that keeps falling down over his eyes. Their mother has put on all her jewelry— bracelets, rings, earrings, necklaces, great heavy pendants made of wrought silver. They glitter in the sunlight.

The spectators gather on the sloping hills above the meadow. Kamel's family is in front so as to have a good view of Kamel and his father who will both be taking part in the many races. Kamel can ride as fast as any of the adults and sometimes he outdistances them, galloping over the meadow like the wind.

The meet ends with a tug-of-war. The prize is a white goat which has just been slaughtered behind one of the yurts. Only the adults take part in this contest, for it is a rough one. The object is to snatch the goat away from the others and ride off with it across the finish

The mounted tug-of-war the Kazaks play uses a white goat as a prize.

line. The contestants tug and pull at the goat, until one of the men breaks loose with the carcass and heads for the finish line, only to be overtaken by someone else before he reaches it. Then the wrangle starts all over again. Finally Kamel's father gains possession of the goat and manages to gallop off with it, outdistancing everyone. Holding up the body triumphantly he crosses the line.

The goat will not be wasted. Kamel's mother will prepare and cook it, and victor and vanquished will all be invited to the feast. The Kazaks are a generous and hospitable people.

Now the time has come to move the sheep to lower pastures, for night frosts are covering the meadows with a white rime, withering the grass. All over the mountains livestock will be on the move. Some ten thousand sheep, great herds of cattle and horses will be descending to escape the approaching winter.

While his father goes off to round up the sheep, Kamel helps his mother and sister with the packing. Kitchen utensils, bundles of clothes, felt carpets, bedding, all are folded and fastened to the backs of the packhorses. Last of all, the yurt is dismantled. First the carpets are removed from the frames, and the frame is broken apart. The carpets are then wrapped around the bare poles and loaded on horses. It takes less than two hours to complete the job.

The family sets off astride their horses, the baby bouncing along in his cradle. Now Kamel joins the other herdsmen, who wear whips stuck handily in their belts. While the women look after the children and keep the laden pack animals moving, the men and boys drive the sheep before them.

On lower meadowlands the yurts are quickly unpacked and set up by the women while the men drive the flocks to pasture. When the men return the meal will be ready.

The brigade plans to stay here until the winter frosts descend and

Moving cattle.

drive them still further down the slopes. However, in these high altitudes seasonal changes can come quickly. Only two weeks after the brigade has set up camp, a mountain blizzard suddenly engulfs the little settlement. When Kamel opens the door flap of the yurt, snow and hail batter his face. The snow begins to pile up against the side of the yurt. At all costs the sheep have to be herded into the shelter of an overhanging cliff. Here, shielded from the wind and huddled together, they can keep each other warm. Otherwise they will freeze to death.

Kamel, his father and mother put on fleece-lined jackets, leather boots, gloves and fur-lined caps. Leaving Biken in charge of the baby, they go out into the driving snow and fight their way to their horses tethered nearby. Soon the family is separated by the blinding white wall into which they can see only a few yards at a time. They have to trust their horses to pick their way through the rapidly growing drifts. It is a lonely unfamiliar world in which Kamel now finds himself.

55

Frosty plumes of icy breath trail from his nose and the horse's flaring nostrils. The horse can hardly walk against the driving wind. It has to be forced along by Kamel's snapping whip.

Under an outcrop of rock Kamel finds two ewes, drowsy with the cold. He rouses them and drives them relentlessly to the sheltered area. Then he leaves to look for more. It is long, dangerous work and night falls before the last sheep are discovered. Two have already frozen to death. Of the 298 left, some are so ill and weak they may not survive the night. But the herders have done all they can. They struggle back to their yurts.

By morning the blizzard has blown itself out. A cold sparkling sun shines down on a white and silver world. All the pasturelands are now buried under some three feet of snow. The men go out to check the sheep and find a dozen more have died during the night. The rest will die of starvation if they stay here. They must be brought down immediately to pasture at levels which the blizzard has not reached. But snow blocks the way and conceals the steep, treacherous mountainside road. It is impossible to move.

Then shortly after noon Kamel hears the sound of a motor approaching from below. The sound grows louder and louder, a great chugging and clanking. The herders cheer as a red snowplow at last comes into view shoving away the snow. The snowplow belongs to the cooperative. It was bought with some of the profits contributed by the various brigades.

The cooperative has proved its worth in another way. Several farming brigades belong to it. While the herdsmen have been tending sheep and cattle in the high pastures, these farming brigades have been raising barley in the lower valleys. Now the barley is reaped and placed in storage sheds to feed the livestock through the winter. In former years the animals had to make do with what scant forage they could find in the icebound lowlands. Many died. Others were weakened and could not produce healthy lambs and calves. Now with the help of the winter fodder, the livestock can be kept healthy.

During the winter months the Kazak herders will also live differently. Instead of yurts their homes will be small adobe houses or caves dug into the foothills. Kamel's family lives in one of the houses. Every day Kamel and Biken along with other brigade children attend school. Their schoolroom is dug out of the cliff face. The teacher is a teenager who has just graduated from an Urumqi middle school.

The cold wintry months pass slowly as, day by day, Kamel studies in school. But often his thoughts stray to the high forests. He longs to be back there with the wind in his face and the flanks of his horse steaming between his knees, as he gallops over the high, wide meadowlands.

THE HUI PEOPLE

Sometimes fourteen-year-old Ma Yao-hua daydreams of the time when her ancestor Burhan Muhammad came over the Old Silk Road to China. Her grandfather, who has a fine imagination, often describes that event for her as if it had happened only yesterday and not centuries ago.

She sees the dust raised by the hooves of the great camel caravans that have set out from Arabia so far away. Day after day, month after month, for a year they travel over wild mountains and through the windswept, murmuring sand dunes of the Taklamakan desert. The camels are laden with goods to be given as tribute to the great emperor of China or sold in the marketplace at the imperial city of Changan.

Ancient Changan stood on the site of present-day Xian (formerly spelled Sian). For 1100 years Chinese emperors ruled from this capital.

During the Western Han dynasty (B.C. 206-A.D. 8) Chinese armies opened up traffic to the west—to Central Asia, to Persia, and finally to the outskirts of the great Roman Empire. Over the newly opened road the traders took silk. Hitherto unknown, silk became the rage of the ladies of Rome, and to get it they poured wealth into the coffers of the Han emperors.

In those days Changan was equal to Rome in world importance. Then both Changan and Rome declined. Changan did not return to its former splendor until the time of the Tang Dynasty (618-907 A.D.) when once again the might of the Chinese Empire was felt around the world. The magnificence of the renewed imperial city, with its great east and west marketplaces, became legendary. It was for the west marketplace that Yao-hua's ancestor was bound with his cargo of spices and jade. It took him a whole year to reach Changan.

There Muhammad lived in one of the hostels built by the government for the use of merchants and envoys during their stay in China. The foreign merchants set up shops in the western market and sold their cargoes of pearls and sea turtle shells, rhinoceros horns, and exotic bird feathers, precious stones, spices, medicinal herbs and handicrafts from their own countries. Chinese shops displayed silks and brocades which the merchants would purchase to take back to the west for sale.

The marketplace was always a riot of color and noise and movement. Streams of horses and carriages passed down the wide tree-lined street. Swarms of pedestrians browsed in the shops or watched the entertainment, because the west market was also the place where foreign managers exhibited their theatrical troupes. Acrobats, jugglers, musicians, singers, dancers, skilled horsemen all put on performances in the hope that the representative of a nobleman or even the emperor would see their acts and engage them to entertain at the palaces.

Muhammad found it very pleasant in the great capital. So when the Chinese emperor extended his welcome and protection to any visitors who wished to remain, Muhammad stayed on in Changan.

Muhammad was a devout Moslem. He read the Koran daily, and daily turned in the direction of Mecca, the holy city, to prostrate himself and say his prayers. Carefully he followed the other regulations of his faith, eating no pork, and eating beef and mutton only if the animal had been butchered in the prescribed way.

These rules were not difficult for Muhammad to follow. Being a well-to-do merchant he had brought along an imam, or Moslem religious leader, who could say the involved religious services and supervise the killing of the animals.

But one strict regulation could not be overcome. By Moslem law Muhammad was not permitted to marry an unbeliever. And there were no Moslem women in China. Muhammad remedied this by buying a baby and bringing her up in the Moslem faith. Patiently he waited until she was of age, and then he married her.

A number of other Moslems who had decided to stay in China were doing the same thing. As their descendants grew up they married one another and the population of Moslems increased. These were the Hui.

Meanwhile as the centuries went by the imperial capital was moved from Changan to Peking. The old Silk Roads fell into disuse as traffic began to come to China by sea. Now traders followed this sea route, selling their wares in the port city of Canton or Guangzhou as it is known in China. Soon a large colony of Arabian Moslems had established itself there.

In later centuries a Moslem community sprang up in Shanghai and a third in Beijing. From these cities as well as from Xian and other places along the Old Silk Route, the Moslem descendants spread throughout China. Many remained in the cities. Others moved to the countryside and took up farming. Everywhere they settled, the Hui built mosques where native imams trained in the Koran conducted religious services.

As the numbers of Hui increased, the Han Chinese began to regard them with increasing hostility. The Hui lived in clannish communities away from the Han Chinese. They followed customs which the Hans could not understand. Most of the Hans were Buddhists or Taoists or Confucianists. Statues of Buddha and his followers, of Lao Tze (the founder of Taoism), or of Confucius, sat behind their altars; scrolls hung in their holy places. Hui mosques were different. They were bare of decoration of any kind.

Other Hui customs were strange to the Hans. A Hui never ate

A mosque used as a museum today.

61

pork or horse or mule meat. The pig—which the Han prized highly—was considered such an unclean animal by the Moslems that they would not even allow its name to be spoken in their presence. This insulted the Hans. The Hui would allow no wine in their homes. They scrupulously followed rituals of cleanliness, such as washing their hands before drawing water from their wells.

Hui dress was also different. The men always wore white skullcaps and the women long gowns and veils that covered most of their faces.

When the Ching Dynasty came to power in 1644 the Ching shared the Hans' growing dislike of the Hui. The Ching were

Cleanliness is important to the Hui.

foreigners themselves—Manchus from the Northeast Region who had conquered China. The Ching were afraid that the clannish Hui would cause them problems, so they set out to kill off the Hui in a series of wholesale massacres. Somehow, the Hui endured.

The Ching Dynasty was not overthrown until 1912, when the Kuomintang republic came to power under Chiang Kai-shek. The policy of exterminating Moslems continued. The Hui fought back in uprisings which were put down with great bloodshed.

Then, in 1949, Communist forces drove the Kuomintang from mainland China onto the island of Taiwan and founded the People's Republic of China. Mao Zedong, chairman of China's Communist Party, became the new government's leader. Relationships between Han and Hui peoples began to improve. The Hui were given the status of a minority nationality, making them one of the largest in China—some six million in all.

Though the older Huis have clung to some of the ancient Islamic practices their dress is very much like that of the Han Chinese today. Only the men's white skullcaps still set them apart. The women wear shirts and pants like Han women. Instead of veils some of the older ones cover their heads with large shoulder-length kerchiefs. The middle-aged women wear white caps while the younger ones go bareheaded.

The Huis look like the Hans. But there are slight differences. The eyes of the Hui are rounder. Sometimes their hair is curly. Their noses may be longer with higher bridges than the Hans. These are all Arab traits, which have been passed down through generation after generation.

Yao-hua's grandfather has a real beak for a nose. He is a kindly old man with a long white beard and twinkling eyes set in his deeply

A grandfatherly Hui.

wrinkled face. Grandmother is plump and jolly. Both she and Grandfather are still very strict Moslems, but their children are not. The grandparents were overjoyed when Yao-hua's oldest sister, who is married to a Moslem tailor and lives nearby, had a baby, their first boy. According to Moslem ritual the imam chants a liturgy over a newborn son and selects his name. But the young parents would not hear of it. They wanted to pick their child's name themselves.

Grandmother and Grandfather had to accept their wishes, but

they were quite upset. At least they had an imam come in to kill the chickens Grandmother was going to cook in celebration of the birth. Correctly killing the animals they eat is still very important to the Hui. The butcher shops in their communities are run by men trained in the Moslem art of slaughtering animals. Hui restaurants follow Moslem rituals in preparing food.

Yao-hua's father and mother run such a restaurant. They serve mutton or chicken slaughtered by an imam, and good fresh vegetables. Xian lies in the center of a large agricultural district, and from nearby fields the grandparents get string beans, squash, taro, and corn. So much corn is grown here that the children walk around eating it off the cob as though it were candy.

Yao-hua likes Sunday best of all the week for that's a school holiday. Workers are free from the factories. Peasants in the outlying fields also have the day off. The streets of Xian are crowded with people shopping or just looking around.

Yao-hua's father likes to take the family on sightseeing excursions when he can close the restaurant for a day. There are so many things to see—the Big Wild Goose Pagoda built in 652 A.D. and the Little Wild Goose Pagoda, built in 707, the Bell Tower which stands in the center of the city. Once there was a sentry to toll the great bell at every watch to inform the citizens that all was well.

One day the family clambers aboard a bus bound for the tomb of Qin Shi Huang Di (formerly spelled Chin Shih Huang Ti), who founded China's first empire (221-210 B.C.). To do this he had to conquer all the petty feudal kingdoms that then existed. His reign was short but he made it possible for the Han emperors who came after him to become a mighty power in the world.

Qin Shi Huang Di's tomb is 131 feet high and covers an area of

Qin Shi Huang Di's tomb—the hill in the background.

some 450 acres. It lies about thirty miles distant from Xian. In 1974, peasants digging wells a short distance from the great burial mound unearthed several lifesize figures of warriors made of pottery. They notified the government and soon a team of archaeologists arrived to do some scientific excavation. The team uncovered a large vault which contained the remains of about 6000 pottery warriors and horses. They found two more burial vaults, which will be opened only after work on the first is completed.

Meanwhile archaeologists are engaged in the painstaking task of assembling the broken shards, or pieces, and reconstructing the figures. To protect them at their work, the first vault has been covered with a great domed structure looking much like an airplane hangar. The hangar also serves as a museum. Visitors can look down at the reconstructed figures and at the archaeologists working among the remains of the others.

Already some 500 warriors and more than twenty horses have been completed. Yao-hua gazes at these stern-looking pottery men clad in knee-length battle tunics, their hair in topknots. The sturdy horses hold their heads high, pulling wooden chariots that have long since rotted away. The cavalrymen, charioteers, chariot warriors, crossbowmen, kneeling archers, all are poised for battle, though the wooden weapons their hands once carried disappeared a long time ago.

Warrior statues found in the tomb and now on display in a museum.

Yao-hua has the eerie feeling that the ghostly, silent throng guarding the emperor will suddenly come to life and drive her and all the tourists out of the tomb. When she turns to leave she seems to feel their stern gaze still boring into her back.

This coming fall the Ma family plans for a big event—a wedding. Yao-hua's other sister, Yao-lien, is about to marry Ting Shao-yun, a young Moslem who lives outside the city in a farming brigade. Yao-lien met Shao-yun when she was sent to his brigade to teach primary school. The young couple are content with the brief civil wedding which has already been performed at the brigade registry office. But both their families want something more traditional, so a second ceremony will be held in the bridegroom's home.

The young couple pick Friday, the Moslem holy day, for the event because this pleases the older people who are sure it will guarantee Allah's protection. However, neither Yao-lien nor Shao-yun want any long ceremony of ritual chanting. The groom's parents have to be content with calling in an imam to kill the chickens and sheep for the bridal feast.

Yao-lien stays with her parents until her second wedding day arrives. Then she puts on the new pink dress her mother has made for her and fastens a blue scarf about her hair.

Some time around noon the groom's mother arrives to escort the bride to the groom's home. A wagon drawn by two horses and driven by an old man wearing a white skullcap draws up in front of the Ma door. Both horses and cart are decorated with bright red tassles and silk ribbons. Shao-yun's mother goes to the door of the Ma home to lead the bride to the wagon. They are followed by the bride's whole family.

Outside Xian they pass through fields of green beans, cabbages and corn where people who are out working turn to look and shout congratulations. Finally they reach the Tings' village. The horses pull up before the Ting doorway. Villagers are lined up on either side of the road to stare at the bride.

Yao-lien feels embarrassed before all those staring eyes. She wonders if she will ever fit in here. And she is relieved when the groom's mother leads her away into the inner courtyard and then to the chamber which Yao-lien will share with her new husband.

The walls of the room have been freshly painted and are decorated with posters of country life. Two bright red wardrobes stand against the wall facing the door. Against another wall stand

Villagers stare at visitors.

three wooden trunks containing the possessions of the new bride. In front of them are piled six new quilts and two new pillows, gifts from the bridegroom's family.

The bed is covered with a bright red spread. The bed is not like the western-style bed Yao-lien has at home. It is a brick platform called a *kang* which has a hollow space underneath. On cold days the kang is heated by a vent from the kitchen stove on the other side of the wall. The vent conveys hot air from the wood- and coal-burning stove to the hollow space, warming the kang, after which it passes outside through a wall chimney.

While Yao-lien rests in her new room, her family exchange traditional Moslem greetings with Mr. Ting: "Salam Alaikum! Salam Alaikum!"

Then they are led into the reception room. It contains twin kangs. On each kang stands a small table seating six people apiece. One is for the male guests, the other for the female ones. Here all day long visitors have been coming in relays to take their turn at the bridal feast. The meal is traditionally Hui. There are dishes of stewed veal, and mutton, gelatin dishes, fried cakes and rice.

Late in the afternoon the horses are harnessed again to bring the Mas home. But Yao-hua has been invited to stay a few days so that she can share in the young people's celebration which will take place this evening.

When twilight deepens into darkness, gay paper lanterns hung in the courtyard send flickering lights and shadows over the faces of the young guests. The bride and groom welcome them with dates and sunflower seeds and candy. Then comes the highlight of the evening. According to custom, the new couple are expected to entertain the guests by singing to them.

The bridegroom has such a terrible voice that no one asks him to

70

sing more than once. But Yao-lien's voice is so clear and sweet that the guests demand song after song from her. Presently she is singing confidently, her cheeks flushed with excitement, her eyes sparkling. Yao-hua realizes that Yao-lien is beginning to feel at home here. And she is happy for her sister.

As the guests leave, the elder Ting strolls into the courtyard.

"A nice party, eh?" he asks Yao-hua. "Though I'm sorry we couldn't have all the rituals, I can tell you I'm glad one old practice has gone. The day after I got married my friends followed the custom of congratulating me by making fun of my father. They painted his face red, hung red peppers on his ears and made him walk down the street wearing his sheepskin coat inside out and carrying a fan. Oh he hated it, but he didn't dare show it. He had to pretend he enjoyed playing the dolt. Thank heaven, I don't have to go through that!"

5

SODO OF INNER MONGOLIA

It is bitter winter on the rolling grasslands of Inner Mongolia. "White sheep blizzards," as they're called, strike with fierce abandon. Howling winds and snow drive across the wide steppes so that fourteen-year-old Sodo, herding stray cattle to shelter, can scarcely see a few feet in front of him.

Sodo is a Mongolian and his people have roamed these vast plains for centuries. He is a robust boy with a sturdy body and a round open face. Beneath a thatch of coal black hair his eyes sparkle. His cheeks glow from winter cold.

Even in his sheepskin jacket and trousers, covered by his huge sheepskin coat, he feels the bite of these freezing winters. Cinched in at the waist with a belt, his coat reaches to his ankles. The sleeves reach almost six inches below his fingertips. Below the wrists these elongated sleeves are made of horsehide. Sheepskin is stiff and unmanageable, but horsehide is flexible so that Sodo can easily grasp things without ever exposing his hands.

Just as Sodo is wearing his winter clothes, so is the little Mongolian horse on which he sits. It has shed its short summer coat of hair for a long thick one. The horse is smaller than other breeds, but it is both hardy and spirited. Sodo rides it bareback because his father feels that's safer than a saddle. If the horse were suddenly to bolt and throw Sodo, the boy might not be able to free his feet from the stirrups. Then, as sometimes happens on the grasslands, he could be dragged for miles. "Better to be thrown free," Father explains. "My brother was killed by being dragged."

In one hand Sodo carries a pole to which a hoop has been attached. Pole and hoop take the place of the western rope or lasso. Whenever Sodo wants to stop a cow from straying, he flings the hoop over its head and pulls it back.

Now at last Sodo gets the cattle to the *kunlun*, an enclosed compound. The tribal unit to which Sodo belongs has built an adobe shed

Rolling grasslands of Inner Mongolia.

at the side of the kunlun. Here fodder has been stored—meadow grass cut last autumn for use in bad weather.

Inner Mongolia, where Sodo lives, was once part of a vast territory which stretched from the province of Kansu in the west to the Northeast Region in the east. To the south it bordered on what was known as China proper. To the north it stretched as far as Siberia.

Here for centuries wild nomad tribes lived under warrior chieftains. Riding their spirited Mongolian horses they would make raids into China, plundering, massacring, or kidnapping the peaceable Chinese farmers. It was to protect his new empire from these nomad tribes that Qin Shi Huang Di built the Great Wall of China, which stretches for some 1500 miles from the coast inland. But the wall did little good when emperors were weak. And in the thirteenth century the Mongol chieftain Kublai Khan conquered China and established his capital in present day Beijing. It was his court that so impressed the Italian traveler Marco Polo.

Today Mongolia is divided into two sections: Outer Mongolia (People's Republic of Mongolia) and Inner Mongolia. Outer Mongolia is officially an independent nation but is actually a satellite of the Soviet Union. Inner Mongolia belongs to China, and is an Autonomous Region. Inner Mongolia is part of the great Mongolian plateau, with an average elevation of 3000 feet. It is an arid to semi-arid country. Grasslands stretch from the Gobi Desert in the west to the Greater Hinggan (Khinghan) mountains in the east.

There are some two million Mongols living in Mongolia and the northwest area of China. Of this number, about 600,000 live in Inner Mongolia; the rest of the population is mostly Han. Sodo lives in the grasslands that lie beyond the Daqing (Daching) mountains. This low range separates the farm and pasture lands to the south from the open grasslands to the north. A pass through the mountains is heavily fortified: beyond the pass the land stretches away in rolling plains to the boundary of Outer Mongolia. Here the Soviet Union has stationed close to a million soldiers and numerous fighter planes.

There are a few farms on the north side of the mountains along with some clusters of adobe houses, their windowless backs turned to the north to shelter the inmates from freezing Arctic blasts. But Sodo lives beyond even these fringes of cultivation. His family is one of seven making up a tightly knit unit which shares flocks of sheep and herds of cattle, goats and horses.

The unit is part of a larger tribal division known as a *Banner*. The headquarters of the Banner are located at an old lamasery north of

Lonely houses dot the landscape.

Huhhot, the capital. The headquarters has a school, a small shopping center and government offices. But Sodo and his family see little of this. Their lives are a cycle of wanderings as they follow the summers northward and flee southward from the winters.

Bold, independent, free, these hearty steppeland nomads live a boisterous life, toughened by the hard conditions which are their heritage. They can be fierce enemies or warm, generous friends. The stranger that appears at the doorways of their yurts will be welcomed inside for a snack of hot milk tea, cheese, deep fried doughnuts, and, of course, kumiss—fermented mare's milk, which has an alcoholic content that ranges from ten to forty percent.

It is of warming kumiss that Sodo is thinking as at last he gets the cows into the kunlun and pitches them some hay. He is hopeful that the blizzard will blow itself out without leaving too much snow behind. Scant snow cover can be scraped away, allowing the cattle to

Commune center.

feed again. But if the snow is too deep, the cattle and sheep will need the stored fodder. If there isn't enough to sustain the 200 or so cattle and the flocks of sheep, the nomads will have to pack their yurts and move southward again. Snow is their worst enemy.

Sodo's yurt looms against the lead-colored sky as the blizzard lets up. The yurt is a great mushroom shape which resembles the Kazak yurts. After the cold of the outer world, the interior of the yurt is comfortably warm. Three heavy felt rugs laid on the ground form the floor. In the center a bucket-shaped stove standing on three legs glows red with an intense fire. The stove, whose chimney goes up through the overhead skylight, warms the yurt and is also used for cooking. The fuel is dried steer manure cakes which are stacked in huge wicker hampers along the sides of the yurt.

Sodo's mother has already cooked the evening meal and is now setting out the food on a low table drawn up to the fire. Mother, Father, Grandfather, Sodo and his four-year-old sister Donghar sit down to eat. There's plenty of food and Sodo is hungry. But first a big drink of the kumiss to warm himself. That is followed by a heaping bowl of noodles made of wheat flour, along with round buns of steamed bread stuffed with mutton. Since the nomads have no farms, their wheat flour and millet is provided by the government in exchange for some of the unit's livestock. The cereals are then rationed out to the members of the unit. In addition, the unit sells some of its livestock and divides the money among its members. Each individual family also owns some livestock, which it can use as it pleases.

There is always plenty of hot milk tea and rock hard cheese squares to go with the noodles and steamed bread. The cheese has to be dipped in the tea to soften it before it can be eaten. Meat is served in great chunks, half-grilled and bloody still. The family eats more meat during the freezing winter months because it provides their bodies with much-needed fuel.

The meal over, the family goes early to bed. No one washes. It is not only too cold for that, but water, always scarce, is even more difficult to obtain in winter when streams have either dried up or frozen. No one even undresses. Sodo just unfastens the belt of his heavy coat and slips his arms out of the loose sleeves. He then folds the sleeves under his head for a pillow.

If Sodo needs to go to the bathroom during the night, he wraps his coat about him and walks about ninety feet outside the yurt. If necessary, he digs a small hole in the ground and squats over it beneath the great frosty canopy of sparkling stars. When he is finished he covers up the hole and rushes back to the yurt.

By this time the fire has died out, and bitter cold fills the room. When Sodo wakes in the morning he finds that the hot, moist air he has breathed out as he slept has condensed on his coat, covering it with a thin layer of ice.

Breakfast is a big bowl of millet boiled in tea milk and served with milk, like the cereal westerners eat. Then it's back into the bitter cold again. Fortunately, winds have scoured the plains of snow and the cattle can feed without any trouble.

How joyfully the spring is welcomed by the nomads! Then the frozen ground thaws, the snow melts away, gentle rains water the land, and the steppes turn green with the reviving grass. And it's time to be on the move again, to the north.

The unit strikes camp, and soon a long line of wooden carts drawn by oxen strings out across the wide steppelands. Every family owns two or three carts. One cart is just a wooden barrel which Sodo's mother has filled with water from the nearby stream. The

Mongolians have to carry water with them everywhere on the grasslands and so they use it carefully. A barrel has to last the family a whole week.

Grandfather and little Donghar ride in another of the carts. The old man is too frail and Donghar too young to sit astride a horse for long distances. All around the two, the family belongings have been stacked: wool felt coverings for the yurt, wool felt carpets for the floor, kitchen utensils. The frame of the yurt is strapped to the outside of the cart. The cart itself is open to the air. But if it should start to rain or snow or if a fierce wind should come up, a movable wooden roof which rises to a peak can be put on top. Then Grandfather and Donghar ride in darkness because their tiny house has no windows. But they don't mind because they are quite snug inside.

The third cart is like the one in which Grandfather and Donghar are sitting. But it is always covered, for it carries the family food supplies and these must be protected from heat as well as cold.

The Mongolians call these *luh-luh carts*. They are small and easy to pull, and the docile oxen that draw them will obey even a child's

Donkey-drawn carts.

command. In desert parts of Inner Mongolia camels are a valuable means of transport, but they are not used in places where oxen will do. A camel can have a vicious temper when roused, and then it will attack even its master.

Sodo helps the other herdsmen drive the cattle. When they reach a good grazing region, they pitch camp again. Now that it is warmer, Sodo's mother spreads only two felt carpets inside the yurt. She leaves the circular patch at the top of the yurt and the doorway flap open so that the spring breeze can flow through. If provisions are needed or the water barrel is empty, she hitches up one of the family oxen and is off to the Banner store or the nearest stream to get what she needs.

Much of the mother's time is now spent milking cows and making cheese. Cows, ewes and goats are all bearing young, and milk is plentiful. Mother boils a great pot of milk until it becomes very thick. Then she spreads it on a flat board and places another board on top. She and Grandfather press down on the upper board, squeezing out all the liquid they can. This leaves a moist sheet of cheese about an inch thick. The cheese is dried immediately. When it reaches the proper consistency, like western-style cheese, Sodo's mother cuts it into squares. Propping the cheese upright between her knees, she holds one end of a thread between her teeth and pulls the other end downward, the thread acting like a wire cheese cutter.

Now when Sodo returns in the evening he gets soft squares of cheese with his meals. But his mother is looking ahead to the time of winter scarcity and so she spreads most of the cheese squares on shallow willow baskets and hangs them outside from the top of the yurt where the sun can bake them. After two to three days the cheese will be rock hard and will last without molding. Mother stores the hard cheese in leather pouches which she hangs from the rafters of the yurt.

Sodo does the same work as a grown man. He helps cows deliver their calves, drives the cattle to watering holes and the best pastures, and rounds up straying cattle. After dark he takes a night watch to protect the livestock from hungry wolves.

While he is herding he may travel five to ten miles a day. His only food then is puffed rice which he carries with him in a pouch hanging from his horse's saddle. Herdsmen have to keep on the move and there's no time to stop and cook.

Sodo snacks on the rice throughout the day, eating it by the handful. Sometimes he puts the rice in the soup he carries with him in a thermos bottle. Sometimes he drops a handful of puffed rice in his milk tea, heavily laced with sugar. Then he drinks it down quickly before the puffed rice gets soggy.

He rides and rides over the limitless rolling steppelands under a glittering blue sky. The winds that blow against him carry the

A land of seemingly limitless steppes.

fragrances of lush grass and wild flowers. Sometimes a Mongolian lark suddenly spirals upward from a hidden hollow, piercing the sky with its sweet haunting melody.

Cantering over the steppes, Sodo joins the lark in song:

> *"White clouds drifting across the blue heavens,*
> *Under the clouds my horse at a gallop;*
> *I brandish my whip in the four directions*
> *And thousands of birds fly up and around.*
> *If somebody asks me, "Where is this place?"*
> *I'll answer proudly, "This is my home."*

6

THE PEOPLES OF SOUTH CHINA

THE ZHUANG

Lin Chao-feng who is seventeen, lives thousands of miles south of China's cold northlands. He has never seen snow or ice or even frost. His home is in subtropical Guangxi (formerly spelled Kwangsi). He is a member of the Zhuang nationality, China's largest minority. There are some eight million Zhuang. Most live in Guangxi. Formerly a province, today the area has been given the status of an Autonomous Region.

The Zhuang look and dress very much like Han Chinese. But they have the same roots as the Dai (See also p. 99) and have their own spoken language, though many of them know Han also.

Chao-feng's home is a tile-roofed, adobe house, one of a cluster that makes up his village. The house has an inner courtyard surrounded by rooms where Chao-feng lives with his parents, aunts, uncles, grandparents and two younger brothers.

The little village is one of a number scattered throughout the wide plain. They are all part of the same farming commune with headquarters in a larger town. A river winds through the plain, barren now except for some dark green groves of litchi and orange trees and some plantations of lighter green papaya and banana trees.

Soon preparations for planting will begin. Tractors or buffaloes will draw plows through the fertile earth breaking the soil. And after the rains, tiny rice plants will be transplanted from their small plots into the flooded fields. As the season progresses, the plains will be transformed into a waving green sea, turning golden in July, when the harvesting will begin and the second crop will be planted. Then the weather, which is so pleasant now, will be hot and humid.

Chao-feng, who has just graduated from the middle school at commune headquarters, is a farmer like the rest of his family. But he has also been given some paramedical training at a nearby hospital and will receive refresher courses from time to time. He can give first aid to the members of his work team and hopes that one day he may go on to medical college.

Chao-feng's two younger brothers attend the village elementary school. But tomorrow there will be no school for the children and no work for the adults because of the Spring Festival holiday. The Zhuangs call Spring Festival "First New Year's Day," since they celebrate two of them. One comes on the first day of the first lunar month, the second on the thirtieth day of the same month. It is called "Late New Year's Day" and is just as important to the Zhuangs as First New Year's Day because it coincides with planting the rice.

Before dawn of First New Year's Day, Chao-feng's mother is up, throwing out all the leftover water in the kitchen. Then she and her sisters-in-law are off to the river with their empty buckets swinging from their shoulders. The women draw fresh buckets of water and bring them back to the house. The Zhuang believe it would be bad luck to use water left over from the old year.

Shortly after Chao-feng's mother returns, the family eats

Everyone brings products to sell at the bazaar.

breakfast and then sets off for the commune headquarters where a bazaar is being held. Father trundles along a wheelbarrow heaped with fresh vegetables picked from the Lin private garden plot—leeks, cabbages, winter melon. Grandmother is bringing the little embroidered children's shoes she has been making all year, while Chaofeng's mother and aunts have embroidered dozens of cloth strips for dress trim. The family will set up a stall and sell their products. It is a fine way to make a little extra money.

People are coming from all the commune villages. Some bring garden produce, some handsewn children's clothes, bamboo baskets, bananas, papayas, oranges. Several men are wheeling along fat live hogs trussed upside down on wheelbarrows. In that position they don't struggle but lie quietly with eyes closed as if enjoying a good nap.

Once they reach the bazaar, Chao-feng leaves his family to stroll around. Handicrafts and farm produce don't interest him. He hurries by rows of plucked chickens and ducks and the carcasses of pigs, all hanging by their legs from overhead racks. Chao-feng finally stops at the stalls where the state department store is displaying goods, all kinds of manufactured things from fabrics and readymade clothes to canned food and farm tools. There are thermos bottles, wristwatches, transistor radios, bicycles. Chao-feng picks up one of the radios and examines it longingly. He would like to own one. But he has not yet saved up enough money for that.

Everywhere there is the chatter and laughter of people on holiday. Cooks standing behind huge pots of boiling oil are frying crullers and pastries of all kinds. On temporary platforms amateur village musicians pluck and bang away at guchins (Chinese fiddles), pipas (lutes), and copper drums. Amateur singers and dancers perform.

Chao-feng joins some former classmates and they wander off from the racket of the bazaar to the sports field outside town. Some young

A pretty, young Zhuang girl.

people have formed teams and are playing on the basketball court. Basketball is very popular all over China today.

The Zhuang game of Throw-the-Embroidered-Ball is just as popular with the Zhuangs as basketball. Chao-feng and his friends hurry to join a game. The ball is a patchwork pillow which the girls have made out of leftover scraps of cloth and stuffed with rice husks. Tassels flutter from the pillow's four corners and one hangs from its bottom. A piece of cord on top serves as a handle. Boundary lines in the form of a square, 164 feet to a side, have been marked out on the ground. The teams line up on opposite boundary lines. Each has a chieftain. Chao-feng is chieftain of his group.

Now the game begins. Back and forth, back and forth the patchwork ball flies. If someone throws it out of bounds or fails to catch it, that side must forfeit a player, who is said to be "captured." If a chieftain himself is captured, the game is over.

At last only the two chieftains are left. The little pillow comes flying high over Chao-feng's head. He jumps—and misses it! He loses and his captors surround him.

"Which do you choose," they ask, "wind or rain?" He thinks an instant. If he chooses wind everyone will be blowing down his neck. If he chooses rain he will be doused with water. But they must catch up with him first.

"Rain," he shouts and takes to his heels, the whole pack of players after him. But only one, a girl, has a bucket of water. Faster and faster he runs, but the girl is close behind. Then his foot turns on a stone and he's down on his knees. And the girl is over him, dumping water on his head. He looks up to see her pretty laughing face. Long shiny black braids hang over her shoulders. A pink hibiscus is tucked over one ear.

Chao-feng scrambles to his feet and the crowd of young people troop back to the bazaar. They are all hungry and cluster like flies around one of the stalls where oversized pyramid-shaped dumplings made of glutinous rice stuffed with pork are set out. They're a favorite delicacy with the Zhuang, and the young people start buying them.

Chao-feng gets one and breaks it in half. He hands one half to the girl who dumped water on him.

"Let's play again on Late New Year's Day," he says.

But the girl doesn't answer. She only laughs and runs away with the dumpling in her hand.

THE YAO

Some 200 miles northeast of the plain where Chao-feng lives are the rugged mountains of the Dayao range. Thirteen-year-old Lung Mei-ying lives in a tile-roofed wooden house in a tiny mountain village which is surrounded by fields stretching down to the banks of the fast-flowing Jinxiu river. Everywhere there is the sound of rushing water as streams plunge down the steep slopes to the lowlands. Though the mountains are not high, they are so rugged that in the past the villagers who lived in different valleys never saw each other and developed different dialects and customs.

Mei-ying is a Yao. There are so many Yaos in these mountains that they have been given an autonomous district of their own, within the Guangxi Autonomous Region of the Zhuang.

More than 2000 years ago Mei-ying's ancestors lived on the plains surrounding the middle Yangtze River. But as more and more Han peasants migrated south, the Yao were shoved back. Finally they were driven into the wild Dayao mountains where no one cared to follow them.

The first Yaos to migrate here took up the best river flats where they built houses of timber and stone and began growing rice. They came to be called the "Long-Haired Yao" because the men wore their hair long and coiled on top of their heads. They were also called the "Mountain Owner Yao" because they laid claim not only to the river flats but also to the stretches of mountain above them, including all the forests, the rivers, and the wildlife there.

The Yao who came later were known as the "Mountain Hopping Yao." When they arrived, all the land had been taken and they had to rent what they used from the Mountain Owner Yao, paying either with produce or labor. They lived a poor life, scratching fields in the mountain slopes where they would cut down some trees, burn off the brush and raise crops of corn. This is known as *slash-and-burn* farming. When the soil became too poor for use they would move on to new areas. The homes of the Mountain Hopping Yao were crude bamboo huts with cracks that let in the damp mountain cold.

Mei-ying's family were Mountain Hopping Yao. Her mother recalls, "We used to go out and gather wild plants and bring them home for Grandmother to cook. We would eat them along with a little corn. We all wore rags. At night we slept on the dirt floor of our huts, crowded together under one ragged quilt to keep warm. One winter your Grandfather caught pneumonia and died."

After the People's Republic of China was founded, the land in the Dayao mountains was divided among all the Yaos. Mei-ying's family and other Mountain Hopping Yaos each received a share. They moved down to the riverbank where they built this village and started planting paddy fields.

Now there's enough to eat in the Lung home and warm clothes to wear. But not all the Mountain Hopping Yaos are this fortunate. Good land in the mountains is scarce, and there isn't enough to go around, so some are still living in the old ways. Even the Yaos who have land are not so well off as the Zhuang and the Han in the plains below.

Nonetheless things are better. Electricity has come to the villages through generators which harness the power of the rivers. Lumbering and collecting oil from the wild tung trees provide other ways of earning a living. Health clinics and a hospital bring free medical services to everyone. And there are many more roads now, so that people in the various villages can visit one another more easily. Young people from formerly isolated valleys can get together and make friends and even marry.

Weeks before Spring Festival arrives in Mei-ying's village, preparations for it are under way. Day and night there's the sound of cow horns blowing, of gongs and drums being beaten. In the compound outside the village the men are slaughtering hogs, chickens, cattle, sheep for the coming feasts. Mei-ying helps her mother and grandmother and older sister, Kuei-jung, make bean curd and glutinous rice pastries and other delicacies.

On the eve of the festival every household sets off firecrackers. There is crackling and snapping everywhere. Mei-ying and her sister shriek with laughter every time they set a long taper to the bunches of firecrackers they have tied to the scaffold which their father has set up well away from the house. The great red crackers explode singly at first and then all at once. Bang! Bang! Bang!

While the girls are having their fun their father is pasting New Year's pictures on the doorjambs. Everything is ready now.

New Year's Day starts early with the roll of the long drums summoning the young people to the open meadow along the river flats. They arrive in their holiday finery. Mei-ying has put on her new dress, but it cannot compare with her older sister's. Kuei-jung's long

Festival time!

Lavishly embroidered gown
and elaborate headdress
adorn this young lady.

91

straight gown is lavishly trimmed with bands of embroidery and she wears an elaborate headdress. Three stiff upright pieces decorated with silver ornaments rise from the crown of her head, giving her a regal look.

The young men are wearing bright red turbans with the plumes of cocks stuck jauntily in them. The boys have been waiting for the girls. Now the folk dancing and singing begin, and everything becomes a shifting kaleidoscope of color.

Mei-ying notices her sister with a handsome young man from another valley. She knows the young man because he has visited their village before and has found many excuses to talk with her sister.

Mei-ying is afraid that soon Kuei-jung will marry the young man and he will take her away to his home on the other side of the mountains. Mei-ying has always felt very close to her sister. She is suddenly filled with sadness and a sense of loss. The New Year that began so joyfully droops heavily about her.

7

THE MIAO AND THE DAI

It's dawn of the Harvest Moon Festival that falls on the fifteenth day of the eighth lunar month—in the western calendar, usually some time in September or October. This is a time of rejoicing. In the small valleys tucked away among forested mountains the rice is ready to be harvested. And tonight the moon will be at its fullest and brightest.

Seventeen-year-old Teng Chung-hsing is practicing on his lusheng. This evening he will serenade his girl-friend. It's the Miao way of inviting her on a date. Chung-hsing is a Miao and the lusheng is the Miao's traditional musical instrument. Almost everyone knows how to play it. And every Miao village has its own lusheng orchestra which performs at weddings and funerals and at all festivals.

The lusheng is made up of eight to sixteen bamboo pipes of different lengths, all fastened to a long mouthpiece. The notes produce a range of tones from loud and strong to soft and sweet. Miao legend says that the first pipes had no holes in them. Then one day rats gnawed through a pipe. When the lusheng-maker played on the pipe he discovered that it produced better tones than the old ones. Today all lusheng-makers put holes in their pipes. And all of them revere rats.

Miao traditional musical instrument, the lusheng.

The Miao people, who look much like Han Chinese, did not always live in such wild mountain regions. Thousands of years ago they were driven out of the plains by the invading Hans. Like the other minorities they fled to the rugged mountains which were too wild and poor to attract the invaders. Here they raised millet and buckwheat by the slash-and-burn method, supplementing their diet with the flesh of domestic animals and wild game. Many Miaos are still slash-and-burn farmers.

Miaos are a scattered minority found in the mountainous regions of the south. Some 2,700,000 live in Yunnan and Kweichow provinces. They also live in the hill country of northern Vietnam and

Laos, which lie across the border from China. Here they go under the name of Hmong.

Wherever the Miaos are gathered in sufficient numbers in China they are given autonomous status. Chung-hsing lives in such an area in Yunnan Province. It is called the Pingbian Autonomous District. His village is in a small valley in the mountainous area that separates Vietnam from China. This rugged land is carved by deep gorges through which rivers rush. Steep, jumbled slopes covered with lush tropical forests overshadow the rivers. A pass through the mountains leads to North Vietnam.

In the 1800s a railroad over the pass was built by the French who ruled Vietnam until 1954. The railroad was modernized in recent times and was used by China to ship war materials and food to North

A group of Miao traveling by boat.

Vietnam during the Vietnamese War. At that time China and Vietnam were friends.

Today, under the influence of the Soviet Union, Vietnam's relationship with China has cooled. Vietnamese soldiers began to make numerous raids on Chinese villages over the border, killing some villagers. China retaliated by sending her armies into Vietnam. Then Vietnam drove all the Chinese out of the country, no matter how long they had lived there. Among them were the Hmong hill people. Many were killed or starved to death. Others left all their possessions behind and fled across the border to China or became boat people seeking asylum.

The border raids still continue. Chung-hsing is a member of the village militia which helps patrol the mountains to keep Vietnamese soldiers from slipping through. The militia are volunteers trained by the Chinese People's Liberation Army. They are given guns and grenades and taught how to use them. In case of outright war they will aid the regular army.

Li Yuan-ying is in Chung-hsing's patrol group. On horseback, the two often ride together on border patrol. Chung-hsing likes the girl very much. It is for her that he will play his lusheng. He hopes she will accept his invitation and join him in the great Harvest Moon song fest. But first there will be dancing in the meadow outside the village. Already the village orchestra is playing and young people are gathering. Laughing girls in their richly embroidered blouses and calf-length skirts come skipping forward, fluttering embroidered ribbons. They tie one end of the ribbon to the waist of a young man. Holding fast to the other end, the girls begin to dance with the partners they have chosen.

A girl ties her ribbon to Chung-hsing's waist and so he has to stay with her. But he would rather be with Yuan-ying, who is merrily

96

Miao girls in festive dress—
headdresses and necklaces
are silver.

dancing with someone else. He wonders unhappily if she will accept his invitation tonight.

Late in the afternoon the young people scatter to their homes where the Harvest Moon feast is awaiting them. Chung-hsing's mother is serving all kinds of Miao dishes. One of the favorites is called "fragrant pig." It is pork that has been cured with rich spices. Roast tea is also very popular. It is made by slowly roasting tea leaves with vegetable oil, salt, spring onions, ginger, peanuts and puffed rice.

The Harvest Moon feast is supposed to be a happy affair, but Chung-hsing's mother is melancholy.

"In the old days we all used to cross the border to celebrate with our relatives," she sighs. "Now the border is closed. We don't even know where they are or if they're still alive."

Chung-hsing feels a moment of sadness too. But it disappears as excitement fills him. At dusk he steals away to Yuan-ying's home. Just outside her window he begins to play—first a trill, then softer notes, then the trill again, very sweet and high.

Suddenly Yuan-ying's laughing face appears at the window.

"Wait a minute," she calls. The next instant she is with him.

Chung-hsing pipes a gay tune on his lusheng as they hurry off to the meadow where the young people are gathering again. Laughing and talking they wait while the sky darkens and a growing night breeze whispers in the trees. Insect voices murmur. Frogs begin to croak.

Then a soft glow appears in the east, and soon the great wheel of the moon bursts above the dark mountain rim. The young people let out a cry as the silvery light floods over them.

"It's time. It's time," voices shout.

Chung-hsing begins to play his lusheng. Others join in. Someone else starts to sing. Soon the whole company, singing and piping, is walking along the winding trail that leads through the forest. In the first clearing they stop to sing before a cluster of houses nestled under a clump of bamboo trees.

Suddenly older people burst out of the houses bringing harvest delicacies, round moon cakes, peanuts, roasted tea. The young people eat, sing their thanks and move on to the next village.

And on and on through the mountains, up, up and around, singing, singing. Occasionally they meet bands of carolers from other villages. The two bands sing greetings to each other. Then on again, village after village while the moon rides higher in the sky.

Hand in hand, Chung-hsing and Yuan-ying move through the

ghostly night bathed in the mysterious silvery moonlight. Happiness floods them, bursting out in waves of melody. Tomorrow they will be back in the workaday world, but tonight it is all magic.

THE DAI

Tao Su-chen lives some two hundred miles to the west of the Pingbian Autonomous District. Here the mountains are higher, rising more than 6500 feet above sea level. They form a barrier between China and Laos and Burma to the south. Su-chen's little village stands in a small valley of paddy fields. Groves of cultivated teak trees and coconut palms, mangoes, and banana trees surround the fields.

Su-chen is a Dai and her people are related to the Thais of Thailand who also look very much like Han Chinese. So many Dai live in this area that it has been made an Autonomous Region. It is called Xi-shuang-banna (Hsi-shuang-panna), which means "twelve rice lands" and it sits astride the Mekong River.

Su-chen's home, like most Dai houses, is made of wood and bamboo and stands on stilts. Part of the space below is given over to pigs and chickens. The rest is storage space. Here the family keeps the farm tools and the pestle and mortar used for pounding rice.

The upper story is divided into four parts. The laundry and other household chores are done on a front verandah where sometimes people like to sit and relax. An open space is reserved for drying grain and clothes. The sleeping-dining area is completely enclosed. It has no windows, but light filters in through spaces between the wall boards. So do drafts which help keep the room cool in summer heat. Winters are not cold—the average temperature year-round is 85°.

The sleeping section is curtained off from the rest of the room. The cooking is done on a central stove. On chilly days the family gathers around the stove for warmth. Meals are served on a low dining table. The stools on which the family sit are lower yet. Generally the food consists of herb-spiced vegetables and vegetables dressed with a currylike sauce. Sometimes there is a little meat cut up into the vegetables. A big bowl of sticky, glutinous rice is always placed under the table. When Su-chen wants a mouthful she just sticks her hand into the bowl, picks up some rice, rolls it into a ball with her fingers, and pops it in her mouth.

Most of the Dai men dress like the Hans, in simple jackets and trousers. Some of the women put on Han-style jackets and pants when they work in the fields because they are more practical. But most of them still prefer their traditional long, brightly colored dresses and the gay towel bandanas which they wind round their heads.

Dai women on their way to the fields.

In the rich subtropical jungles above the little valley live many exotic creatures—peacocks, the peafowl and hornbill, rare Asian elephants and panthers, the slow loris, chattering langurs and gibbons. Sometimes the deep bellow of the gaur—the East Indian ox—floats down from the hilly grasslands above the monsoon forests. Because there are so many rare species in these mountains the government has set up a nature reserve here.

Su-chen's grandfather is a *tsanha*, or ballad singer. When he was young, tribal chieftains ruled the villages of Hsi-shuang-panna, which were all very poor and backward. There were frequent cholera, typhoid, and bubonic plague epidemics. But the most prevalent illness was malaria. From May to October warm, heavy rains fall here. Then water fills ponds, paddy fields, and swamps and makes puddles everywhere. These are all excellent breeding grounds for malaria-bearing mosquitoes. Malaria causes chills and fevers. Children who have it become thin and very yellow. Their stomachs swell. Finally they die.

When the village chieftain's only son sickened and died, the witch doctor, who did not like Grandfather's popularity as a ballad singer, accused him of being a pipa devil who had caused the child's death. Grandfather was driven from the village and had to wander through the forests eating wild fruits and digging up roots and doing some slash-and-burn farming. Here he met and married a young girl who had also been driven from her village as a pipa devil.

After the People's Republic of China was founded, the chieftains and the witch doctors lost their power. The land was divided among everyone and the "pipa devils" were called back to the villages. At the same time medical teams began visiting the area with advice about hygiene. They gave inoculations and vaccinations. They helped the villagers drain the ponds and swamps or spray them with insecticides.

They distributed antimalarial medicine, and put mosquito nettings around the children's beds. And so malaria, along with many other diseases, was brought under control.

As March turns into April, the world of Xi-shuang-banna (the new spelling) bursts into bloom. Bougainvillea vines of pink, purple and yellow blossoms trail to the ground in great nets of color. Bell-shaped fuchsias and delicate wild azaleas and camellias liven the dark forests with a riot of color—deep reds, scarlets, silvery pinks, creamy whites. Huge butterflies the size of a man's head float lazily by. Coming back from work in the fields one day Su-chen sees a pair of courting peacocks. The cock, its tail spread, is doing a mincing dance step while a drab hen looks on. It's as though the whole world is preparing for the Water Splash Festival, which always falls around mid-April just before the monsoon rains begin.

Finally the day arrives. The men change their everyday trousers and shirts for traditional holiday dress of tunics and tight pants. They wind silk turbans around their heads. The women put on their brocade, ankle-length skirts and gaily colored blouses. Grandmother wears a bright cotton turban. But Su-chen and her mother pin up their shiny black hair, holding it in place with red combs.

The family sets out for the Lantsang River where the festival is being held. Soon they are joined by other villagers. Everyone is carrying a bowl or a mug or even a bucket. And everyone is laughing and chattering away.

Already crowds are gathering on the river flats. Soon thousands of people will be swarming everywhere. On the river bank, dragon boat teams are preparing to launch their boats for the traditional

Dai women dressed for Water Splash Festival.

races. In the old days people believed that if a woman even came near a boat it would overturn. Now times have changed and there are women's teams too.

Su-chen does not want to watch the races. She lingers to listen to

The boat races are traditional, but women crews are something new.

Grandfather tell the legend of the Water Splash Festival. Once long ago, Grandfather sings, the Dais were ruled by a terrible fire demon whom no one could destroy. Then seven young girls discovered how to kill him. One day when he was asleep, they pulled out one of his hairs and wound it round his neck. Off came his head and rolled away. But everywhere it went it started a fire. Soon fields and forests and villages were all destroyed. The Lantsang River dried up.

The girls put an end to the fires by picking up the head and taking turns carrying it. It began to burn them, but the people ran to their rescue by pouring water over them.

"So now we splash one another in honor of the seven girls, and to celebrate the demon's end," Grandfather sings.

Su-chen hurries on. She makes her way past a group of young men with broadswords who are doing a sword dance. Two men, wearing smiling masks under their bright orange headdresses, are performing the good luck and happiness peacock dance. Su-chen does not stop to watch them either.

Her destination is the sloping grassy bank of the Lantsang River. Here crowds of old and young, even little children, are dipping up water in the containers they have brought with them. Su-chen fills her basin too and then joins a merry crowd that is moving to the rhythms of gongs and elephant-foot drums.

The dancers wind their way along the Lantsang River, through groves of palm and litchi trees, over open meadowlands. As they dance they dip their hands in the sloshing water they are carrying and splash one another, crying out good wishes.

When their water containers are empty the dancers break away and run to the river to fill them again. Then they rejoin the fun, which is getting wilder and wilder. People are beginning to dump whole bucketfuls on one another. Soon everyone is soaked. Su-chen's dress clings wetly to her slender body. Her hair has broken loose from its comb and is streaming down her back. A young man calls out that she certainly looks like one of the beautiful maidens who carried the head of the demon. Laughing mischievously Su-chen dumps her water over his head, refills her bowl, splashes and splashes some more.

All at once black clouds sweep overhead. The sun disappears. Rain pours down, dousing dancers and dragon boat racers and ballad singers. Who cares? Even the thunderstorm is a sign of good luck. It means that the monsoons are coming, that paddy fields will soon be ready for planting, that another rich harvest of rice is on the way.

Water Splash Festival.

8

THE YI

In April, just before the time of the spring plowing, seventeen-year-old Jeke Dachi accompanies his grandfather on the old man's pilgrimage to Headcutting Crag. It stands high in the Daliang shan, the Great Cool Mountains, in southern Sichuan (Szechwan) province.

Dachi has gone with his grandfather every year since he was old enough to walk. Now Grandfather's legs are giving out and he needs a cane, but he still makes the pilgrimage.

The way leads along steep trails over great buttresses thick with virgin forests. High above, tier on tier, snowclad peaks ring them round. There's an early morning chill in the air. Grandfather clutches his old-fashioned heavy black woolen cape about him. It is the traditional garment of the Yi, though the younger men no longer wear it.

Grandfather is old-fashioned in other ways. He still shaves his head except for a patch of hair about three inches in diameter which grows on top of his head. The stiff topknot of hair rises like a horn from the center of the turban he wears.

Dachi is a modern Yi. He wears shirt, padded jacket and trousers. Dressed as he is, he might pass for a Han at first glance. It is only his nose, which is longer and sharper, with a high bridge, that gives him away. He is also taller than most Hans. His father, mother and grand-father are all tall.

It is noon and the weather has turned quite warm by the time Grandfather reaches his destination—a steep clifflike slope on which is carved in Yi characters: Headcutting Crag.

"Here is where my brother, your great-uncle, was beheaded," he tells Dachi, "because he offended his master."

A short distance away another tablet stands over a deep gash in the ground. The tablet reads: Ditch of Blood and Tears. A third tablet set in front of a tree reads: Heartbreak Tree. Several other old men have gathered here. They begin to talk with Grandfather about the past. The relatives of some lie in the Ditch of Blood and Tears. They were buried alive. Others were hanged on Heartbreak Tree.

The old men are emancipated Yi slaves. Three times a year they gather at this gloomy place to recall the terrible past and vow again never to forget it. Each year their numbers dwindle as more of the men die. But to those who remain, the past is as vivid as ever. Dachi knows it by heart. He has heard the story so many times from Grand-father.

Before the founding of the People's Republic of China the Yi of Daliang shan were a slave society. The slave owners were the aristo-crats, the Black Yi. They made up five percent of the people. The rest were known as the White Yi. They were either serfs or slaves.

The Black Yi lived in house forts with high towers, surrounded by bodyguards. The White Yi did all the work. They cultivated the fields of buckwheat, corn, potatoes and yams by the slash-and-burn method. They tended the cattle, sheep and goats. They fought the battles of the Yi chieftains. Their homes were only caves or hovels.

The White Yi slaves had no rights at all. They could not choose their own marriage partners, or raise their own children or even own their own bodies. They could be sold or killed as their masters chose.

The serfs were a little better off, but they also had little freedom. They had to remain on the land on which they were born. If they fell into debt to a Black Yi they could be sold, either as a whole family or separately, to pay off their debts. Then they would become slaves, too.

There are more than three million Yi in China. 120,000 live in Sichuan Province and most of these live in the Daliang shan where they have their own Autonomous Region. Historians believe that in neolithic times the Yi migrated to Yunnan from the source of the Yellow River in the lofty Qinghai (Chinghai) plateau. Many centuries later they came into conflict with the early Han soldiers and were driven into the Great Cool Mountains, the Daliang shan. Here they lived in isolation and developed their unique slave culture.

After the founding of the People's Republic of China, slaves and serfs were freed. The power of the Black Yis was taken away. The government helped the Yi build tile-roofed houses. Wherever possible, families separated by the Black Yi were reunited. Agricultural experts came to teach the Yi how to cultivate the flats along the riverbeds and the lower slopes of the mountains.

It was difficult at first for the Yi to adjust. They had never been real farmers and they had much to learn. The work was hard because even in the valleys the land had to be cleared of rocks and rubble.

But, bit by bit, the Yi learned how to work together to create fields in which they could plant two crops a year, one of rice and one of winter wheat. They formed brigades and then communes. Today most of the communes own at least a few tractors and seed trans-planters to make the work easier. But human beings and draught animals still do most of the work.

108

Yi women in the fields.

Above the river flats terraced fields cling to the mountain's lower flanks. Higher up there are orchards of apple, walnut and chestnut trees. Still higher grow thick copses of cultivated tung trees from whose nuts the Yi extract a valuable oil.

On the hills beyond the river a small flock of sheep and one of goats grazes. Below there is a little herd of cattle, many of them buffaloes used for plowing. Private vegetable gardens surround the little villages. Before, the Yi hardly knew what a vegetable was.

The Yi began to build their own hydroelectric stations to harness the power of the rivers. Today most villages have electric light. Those which do not as yet, use resin lamps or blazing pine chips placed in a pan which is tied to a bamboo pole and raised aloft. New highways

Terraced plantings on the mountainside.

and mountain paths make travel easier. In some places stone bridges have taken the place of the old rickety ones of bamboo.

In 1970 the Chengde-Kunming Railway line was built, the rails cutting through the Daliang shan north to south. The Yi call it their "Road to Happiness" because the train brings them many luxuries—

colorful cotton materials, silk handkerchiefs, earrings, hairpins, patterned lace, velvet, all of which can now be bought in the commune stores.

As Dachi and his grandfather descend into the valley, black clouds sweep over the sky and a storm bursts upon them. Grandfather huddles gratefully under his heavy cape. Dachi hunches his shoulders and the two make for the shelter of their little home. Tomorrow, they know, the rice paddies will be wet enough for planting. All hands will be needed then. And Dachi, who is in high school, will be released with his classmates to help until the young rice seedlings are in.

Dachi is an honor student in the high school which he attends. His lessons are in both Han Chinese and Yi. The Yis have had their own written language for many centuries. It looks much the same as the Han ideograms, but actually it is quite different.

Dachi will graduate this summer. The following fall his life will take a different course from that of his classmates, who will become full-fledged farmers. He has been chosen by the people of his commune and his teachers to attend the National Minorities Institute in faraway Chengde, the capital of Sichuan Province. He has shown such aptitude for animal care and breeding that he is to be given a thorough grounding in the subject. When he returns to his mountain village he will be able to teach others new methods of animal husbandry.

After the plowing and planting Dachi and his classmates return to their lessons. Day by day, week by week, the rows of tiny rice shoots in the fields grow tall. The valley becomes a sea of rippling green and then ripens to a carpet of dull gold as it comes close to harvest time. Every commune celebrates the harvest with a traditional Torch Festival that falls on the twenty-fourth day of the sixth lunar month—August or September in the western calendar. The most

The Torch Festival.

lavish celebration of all is at the county seat of Butuo County. Here there will be wrestling, bullfights, goatfights, horse racing.

The day dawns warm and the great snow-covered shoulders of the mountains stand out sharply against the bright blue sky. The whole family puts on festival clothes.

Dachi and his father wear long trousers and tight black jackets with embroidered lapels and wristbands. In their left earlobes they wear an earring made of three beads—one yellow and two red. Dachi will go bareheaded, but his father puts on the traditional black turban with a hornlike twist on the right. This symbolizes heroism. He has been chosen by his brigade to represent them in the wrestling matches.

Dachi's mother wears a lavishly embroidered bolero-style jacket and a floor-length red pleated skirt. A black cotton headdress crowns her pinned-up hair. She wears strings of beads in both ears and several silver bracelets on both arms.

Now she brings out the family heirloom—the wooden drinking bowl and wooden cups and ladle painted with traditional designs. In the early days people used only wooden bowls which they carved themselves out of pieces of hardwood. Today the Yi use pottery for

Yi women in lavish festival clothes.

their everyday needs. But on festival days they go back to their traditional ways. Father fills the drinking bowl with a fiery white liquor. He begins to ladle it out into the cups which he hands around to his family. It would be considered very rude to refuse to drink a toast at Torch Festival time, so Dachi gulps down the fiery stuff and feels it burn all the way to his stomach.

Presently friends of the family begin dropping in and everyone of them drinks a toast with Father and Grandfather and Mother. This is only the beginning. There will be many more toasts during the day and evening as Father meets friends and acquaintances and even strangers in the county town which the family will soon be visiting. The liquor store in town will be doing a brisk business.

Finally the family sets off, carrying among them some chicken dishes Mother has prepared for a picnic feast. Hundreds of other holidaymakers join them, walking briskly along the mountain paths. The road is full of colors—blue, green, red, white, gold, as all the women are dressed like Mother and most of the men like Father and Dachi.

The town is a beehive of activity. Children race through the streets. Music is being played lustily on pipes that somewhat resemble bagpipes. Voices are raised in laughter, in song, in shouted toasts.

Both sides of the streets are lined with goods displayed in stalls or spread out on the ground. Chickens, piglets, apples, peppers, and vegetables are being sold. Artisans entice the women with displays of wrought silver rings, earrings, necklaces and buttons the size of cats' eyes which they have fashioned themselves.

Mother lingers to examine the jewelry. Grandfather joins a group of elderly ex-slaves clustered on a street corner. Father hurries for the wrestling ring around which a crowd is already gathered. Dachi goes with his father to watch him match his strength against others.

Dachi's father lasts to the very end, but finally he's defeated. The winner struts around the arena holding a long length of red silk aloft. It is his prize.

Dachi makes his way to the place where the bullfights are being held. Every commune has contributed its fiercest bulls for this event. The competing bulls are matched in pairs. The minute they are loosed they begin to fight. Each fight lasts about fifteen to twenty minutes. A volunteer referee decides the winner. When the champion bull emerges he will be paraded through the town with a piece of red silk on his head. For generations bullfights have been a way of choosing fine stud animals that will be used only for breeding purposes.

As the day wears on, families prepare for their picnic feast. Every

Bullfights to choose the best bulls.

brigade has brought its own big pot of meat cuts from the communal animals which have been butchered for the occasion. Each person in the brigade will receive an allotment of four and a half pounds of this meat.

Father joins the line in front of the table where his brigade is stationed. He collects the family share, eighteen pounds of beef in all. He also buys one of the piglets. While Mother stakes out a place for the family to gather, Father finds an open space away from the people and builds a bonfire where he begins to roast the meat. All over the mountain slopes little wisps of white smoke rise from other clearings as beef, mutton, or pork is roasted. In the late afternoon the family gathers for the feast. Their excited voices rise as they glance at the sky from time to time. The big event of the festival will take place after dark.

Finally the sun disappears over the high shoulders of the mountains. As dusk comes, a ripple of anticipation sweeps through the throngs.

Suddenly, numerous lights appear high in the dark shadows of the mountains. The lights look like a fiery dragon. The dragon weaves its way through the thick woods, appearing and disappearing as it descends closer and closer to the valley.

At last the fiery dragon reveals itself as a long procession of people bearing five- to six-foot-high torches. They burst into the plain followed by huge crowds of people all shouting, "Wuyi! Wuyi! Wuyi!" Everyone jumps up to follow the dragon, singing now with a thousand voices:

"*The stars are high in the sky over our mountains.
Oh torches, light up our village.*"

The procession bearing the torches stops in the bullfight arena. It begins to form different designs—a ring, an umbrella, a rectangle.

"Wuyi! Wuyi! Wuyi!" the roar goes up as each new design appears.

Dachi watches wistfully. Next year at this time he will be at the Institute of Minorities in Chengde. Part of him is looking forward to the new experience. But the greater part wishes he could stay behind here in these familiar mountains thrilling to the cries of his people:

"Wuyi! Wuyi! Wuyi!"

9

THE INSTITUTE OF NATIONAL MINORITIES

Dachi boards the train at the Kanlo station which stands between two tunnels in the Daliang mountains. With a melancholy whistle the train is soon on its way. And from the window Dachi waves goodbye to his parents and grandfather who have come to see him off.

They are very proud that their son has been selected to go to the Institute of National Minorities, but they will miss him too. Dachi remembers their sad faces long after the train has left them far behind. Waves of homesickness wash over him. This will be the first time in his life he has left his family and these mountains.

Again and again the spectacular view from the train is lost as the train speeds through long tunnels black as midnight. There are many of these tunnels because it is the only way the train can thread its way through the precipitous mountains. The land here is so steep that in some places the stations themselves are located in a tunnel.

At last the train emerges from the mountains and enters the Red Basin of Sichuan. The broad plain is broken by terraced hills, creased by rivers and dotted by ponds. It is a well-watered land. Though its average elevation is about 2000 feet, the high mountains hold in the air and it is hot and humid.

After seven hours the train finally draws in to Chengde station. Dachi suddenly finds himself filled with apprehension. What if no one is here to meet him? What will he do? Where will he go?

He need not have worried. A young Yi is coming forward, hand extended in greeting. He leads Dachi to the car the school has provided.

"I know how you feel," the young man says, laughing. "I came out of the mountains last year myself. You'll get used to it though."

Dachi wonders if he ever will when he arrives at the complex of Institute buildings on their spacious grounds. He has never seen any like them before—so large and imposing.

His new friend leads him across campus to the dormitories. Here

An Institute building.

he will bunk in a small room with three other young men. In the dormitories he is surrounded by students and teachers all there to greet and welcome him. Dachi is beginning to feel more and more at ease.

At mealtime he is amazed to be served the kind of dishes his mother makes at home. He learns from his friend that every nationality at school is given the food to which it is accustomed. The Moslems have a separate dining room with a special chef who knows the dietary laws.

In the days that follow, Dachi meets many other students. There are close to 2000: Yi, Tibetans, Huis, Miaos, Zhuangs, Mongolians, Dais and Hans. More than 300 teachers and staff members take care of the students. The head of the school is a Han. His assistant is Tibetan.

The Institute of National Minorities in Chengde is one of nine such institutes which are scattered around the country. The students who are brought to each of them have been chosen for their conscientiousness and abilities. The government pays their fares and their tuition. Room, meals and medical care are all free. In addition, each student receives a small monthly allowance.

There are four departments at the Institute: Politics and History; Language and Literature; Mathematics, Physics and Chemistry; Veterinary Medicine and Animal Husbandry. Students who have just graduated from high school attend preparatory classes to enable them to pass the stiff entrance examinations and go on to the college for which they are best suited. Dachi will attend the veterinary department here at the Institute. His friend will go the Chengde Medical College.

Classes at the Institute are held six days a week, but Saturday afternoon is always a relaxed time, for Sunday is a free day. In Dachi's last period the students play a game called "Pass the Pompom." They

120

Class seems to be fun.

sit behind long tables that line the four sides of their classroom. Their young teacher stands at one end. Behind her, a student with his back to the class sits in front of a big drum, holding drumsticks.

At a signal from the teacher he begins to beat the drum while the students pass the pompom from hand to hand, faster and faster, tense and giggling. Suddenly the drummer stops, catching a student with the pompom. The student is penalized by having to sing a song, perhaps play a piece on a flute, or do a little dance. Hilarious laughter and applause break out after each performance, no matter how poor it might be. It's a good game for breaking the ice and making the young people feel at home. Everyone is in good spirits when school breaks up for the week.

This leaves time for Dachi to do some domestic chores. He helps his roommates clean up their sleeping quarters. He scrubs his clothes by hand in one of the big scrub basins which are set on long trestles outdoors. Other students are doing the same thing or cleaning their sneakers while waiting their turn.

When Dachi is finished washing, he hangs his wet clothes out to dry on a long bamboo pole protruding from his dormitory window. Drying them stretched out like that means they will not have to be ironed. Now he has free time till Monday. On Sunday he will go with his new friends to visit the city of Chengde.

October first is a holiday that no one in China ignores. It celebrates the Revolution of 1911 when the Manchus were swept from

Washing clothes, and general cleanup time!

the throne and a republic was founded. It is the equivalent of the Fourth of July in the United States. In the dormitories there is great excitement as the students put on their national costumes, new ones made to order for them by Chengde tailors and paid for by the government.

There is going to be a performance by some of the students who are majoring in song, dance and instrumental music. Around the wide grassy compound where it will take place a crowd is gathering.

The National Minority Institute's orchestra begins to play and the show begins. The first number is a lively dance by Tibetan teenagers. It is followed by young Mongolian men and women in belted tunics or long gowns who stomp and leap, prance and glide in

A performance at the Institute of National Minorities.

movements that resemble the spirited cavorting of Mongolian horses. Then a Dai girl sings a song. She is followed by a Yi. And Dachi hears again the haunting torchlight ballad:

"The stars are high in the sky over our mountains.
Oh torches, light up our village . . ."

Dachi remembers the flaming torches of his faraway home, the roar of *Wuyi! Wuyi!*, the faces of his parents and grandfather as they bade him goodbye. How far away it all seems now! How homesick he feels! For one moment he thinks of going home. He is free to do so if he chooses. But then he remembers why he has come—to help his people lead a better life. And he knows that he will stay.

In the midst of the laughter and applause Dachi shouts at the top of his lungs, "Wuyi! Wuyi! Wuyi!" It is a cry of triumph.

INDEX